The Blackbirch Visual Encyclopedia

Ancient History

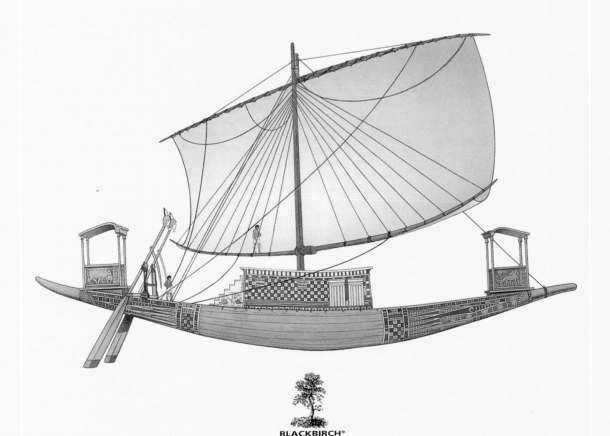

BLACKBIRCH®
PRESS

THOMSON

GALE

San Diego • Detroit • New York • San Francisco • Cleveland • New Haven, Conn. • Waterville, Maine • London • Munich

CONTENTS

THOMSON

GALE

© 2002 by Blackbirch Press™. Blackbirch Press™ is an imprint of The Gale Group, Inc., a division of Thomson Learning, Inc.

Blackbirch Press™ and Thomson Learning™ are trademarks used herein under license.

For more information, contact
The Gale Group, Inc.
27500 Drake Rd.
Farmington Hills, MI 48331-3535
Or you can visit our Internet site at http://www.gale.com

Copyright © 2000 Orpheus Books Ltd. Created and produced by Nicholas Harris, Joanna Turner, and Claire Aston, Orpheus Books Ltd.

Text credit: Jacqueline Dineen,

Consultant credit: Dr. Robert Peberdy

Illustration credit: David Bergen, Simone Boni, Stephen Conlin, Ferruccio Cucchiarini, Giuliano Fornari, Luigi Galante, Andrea Ricciardi di Gaudesi, Gary Hincks, Shane Marsh, Steve Noon, Nicki Palin, Alessandro Rabatti, Rosanna Rea, Claudia Saraceni, Alan Weston

LIBRARY OF CONGRESS CATALOGING-IN-PUBLICATION DATA

Harris, Nicholas, 1956-
Ancient history / Nicholas Harris.
    p. cm. — (Blackbirch visual encyclopedia)
  Includes index.
  Summary: A visual encyclopedia of early humans, first civilizations, and ancient cultures throughout the world.
  ISBN 1-56711-519-5 (lib. bdg. : alk. paper)
    1. History, Ancient—Juvenile literature. 2. Civilization, Ancient—Juvenile literature. [1. History, Ancient—Encyclopedias. 2. Civilization, Ancient—Encyclopedias.] I. Title. II. Series.
D59.H37 2002
930—dc21   2002018656

Printed in Singapore
10 9 8 7 6 5 4 3 2 1

Abbreviations: BC before Christ; AD anno Domini ("in the year of the Lord", indicating years numbered from the birth of Christ); *c.* circa ("about")

CONTENTS

ARCHAEOLOGY

ARCHAEOLOGISTS find out about the past by excavating (digging up) the sites of ancient buildings or settlements. They study artifacts such as tools and pottery to piece together a picture of everyday life in the past.

People have always been curious about the past, but for centuries most people's knowledge of early history came from myths and legends. They did not begin to search for real evidence until the late 18th and 19th centuries, when rich Europeans began to travel and collect curiosities from the ancient world.

Evidence was easy enough to find in Greece and Rome, where buildings and sculptures were there for all to see. But in the Middle East, for example, whole cities lay buried deep in the earth until Europeans began to search for objects from the past.

This tiny ivory head of a young girl, which was found at Brassempouy in France, may be the earliest known portrait in the world. Just under 2 inches (4 cm) high, it was carved over 24,000 years ago. Evidence like this can tell archaeologists a great deal about the past and how people lived and worked.

Once this search for the past had started to take a hold, the first archaeologists began to travel to different parts of the world in search of evidence. They studied clues, such as descriptions in literature, to discover where lost cities might be and then dug down to find them. They uncovered artifacts that had lain there for centuries. Unfortunately some of these were damaged because these early explorers did not have the knowledge that archaeologists have today. But they did make significant discoveries about early civilizations.

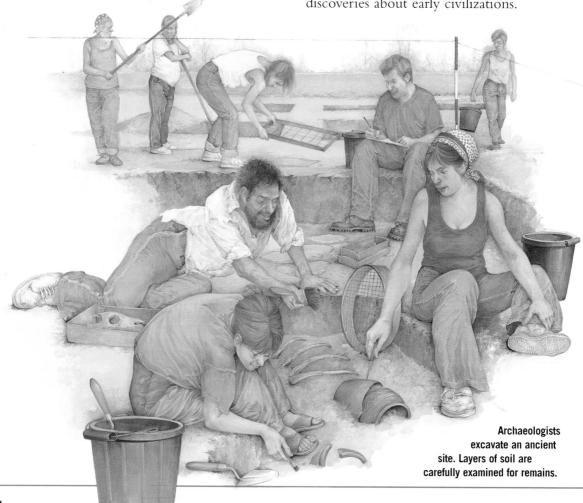

Archaeologists excavate an ancient site. Layers of soil are carefully examined for remains.

Archaeologists have also helped to trace the history of writing with finds such as clay tablets containing ancient scripts. One example of such a find is the library of the Assyrian king, Assurbanipal, who reigned in the seventh century B.C. *(see page 28)*. The library contained 20,000 tablets in an early form of writing. When alphabets such as this were deciphered, people could read ancient historical records which told them more about how the different civilizations lived and organized their communities.

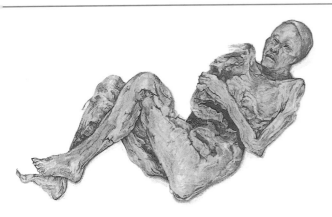

The remains of human bodies give information about diet and disease. The body of this woman has been perfectly preserved by the acid in the peat bog where she was found.

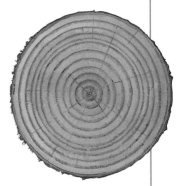

Every year, a tree grows a new layer of bark and sapwood. When the tree is cut down, the layers of sapwood can be seen as single rings. If you count the rings, you can tell the age of the tree. This technique is also used to date wooden objects.

One of the early archaeologists was the German businessman Heinrich Schliemann (1822–1890). He studied two long poems, the *Iliad* and the *Odyssey*, by the Greek poet Homer, in which two lost cities, Troy and Mycenae, are described. Schliemann decided to use the evidence in the poems to search for the two cities. In 1870 he discovered Troy near the Dardanelles in Asia Minor. He found the hilltop fortified town of Mycenae in 1876. He also came across huge amounts of gold at Mycenae, showing that this early Greek civilization was fabulously wealthy *(see page 32)*.

Today, archaeologists can make very accurate assessments of their finds. For example, they can use scientific methods to calculate how old things are. Without archaeologists, we would have only a very sketchy knowledge of history, and the lost cities of the ancient world would have stayed buried forever.

In 1922 a British archaeologist, Howard Carter, made a stunning discovery. He had set out to search for the tomb of the Egyptian boy king, Tutankhamun *(see page 21)*. One morning in November, he and Lord Caernarfon, who had financed the search, found it. Unlike the tombs of other Egyptian pharaohs, grave robbers had not discovered it and all the burial treasures were still there. The king was wearing a fabulous gold mask and his mummy lay in three gold coffins, one inside the other. In a separate chamber were all the possessions he might need in the afterlife.

EARLY HUMANS

THE FIRST EVIDENCE of humanlike
creatures, or hominids, dates back more than
4 million years. Remains of apelike
creatures, called Australopithecines
("southern apes"), have been found in
various parts of Africa. The skeleton of one,
found at Hadar in Ethiopia in 1974, was
named "Lucy" (it was later found to be a
male). Scientists could tell that Lucy,
although it had a chimpanzee-like posture,
stood upright and walked on two feet—the
distinguishing feature of a hominid.

Humans, apes, and monkeys are all
descended from one ancestor. This may have
been *Aegyptopithecus,* or "Egyptian Ape." It
lived in Egypt about 35 million years ago,
climbing through the trees on all fours. Of
all the descendants of this tiny mammal,
only humans developed bipedalism, the
ability to walk upright and on two feet.

Aegyptopithecus

Bipedalism allowed hominids to develop
in an important way that was different from
other mammals. They could use their hands
for other tasks. By about 2.5 million years
ago, *Homo habilis* ("handy man") had
appeared in Africa. It was probably the first
true human, although it still looked apelike. *Homo habilis* could use simple stone
tools, rather than its teeth or its bare hands,
to kill and skin animals for food. The tools
were made by striking one stone against
another to make a sharp edge. These early
pebble tools are so simple that they look
like naturally chipped stones.

**Australopithecines
looked apelike but
walked upright.
They were 3 to 5
feet (1 to 1.5 m)
tall, had long arms
and short legs,
and had a small
brain in a low-
browed skull.**

*Homo habilis
(right)* was
probably the first
true human.

DISCOVERING FIRE

Chewing raw meat must have been hard work but it was thousands of years before early humans were able to soften their food by cooking it. Early humans may have discovered fire by seeing how lightning sometimes set bushes alight. A more intelligent species of human, *Homo erectus* or "upright man," first appeared in Africa about 1.8 million years ago. Taller, leaner, and able to move more quickly across open grassland, *Homo erectus* learned to hunt larger animals with sharper weapons. It was the first hominid to leave the African continent and travel north and east. Remains have been found in China, Java, and Europe. *Homo erectus* had protruding jaws and thick brow ridges, but lived in groups and cooked food over a fire.

Homo erectus males went out hunting while the females gathered plant food and looked after their young. Bones found at the site of one of their camps in China show that they hunted and killed elephants, rhinoceros, horses, bison, water buffalo, camels, wild boar, sheep, and antelopes. The hunters could not have caught and killed large animals like these with simple weapons unless they had a larger and more cunning brain than their ancestors. *Homo erectus* may even have been capable of simple speech, although it still had heavy jaws which had developed for chewing raw meat.

The hunter-gatherers were always on the move. At night, they slept in caves or built simple shelters from branches and skins. The females collected firewood so that they could light a fire to keep themselves warm and cook their food. The males made stone tools, including the hand ax, which could be used for cutting up meat.

China, 500,000 years ago. A *Homo erectus* group sets up camp for the night. A fire has been lit and food cut up for cooking. The fire also helps to keep wild animals away.

HOMO SAPIENS

MORE MODERN-looking people began to appear about 750,000 years ago. These were early *Homo sapiens* ("wise man"). Remains have been found in Africa, Europe, and Asia. Some scientists believe that *Homo erectus* developed into *Homo sapiens* on different continents, but most say that *Homo sapiens* spread out of Africa.

Modern people, given the scientific name *Homo sapiens sapiens*, first appeared about 125,000 years ago, reaching Europe 40,000 years ago. They no longer had the jutting brows and large jaws of earlier *Homo sapiens*, but high foreheads and bony chins. Their brains were larger than any of their ancestors, apart from the Neanderthals. They have been the only humans on Earth since the Neanderthals disappeared.

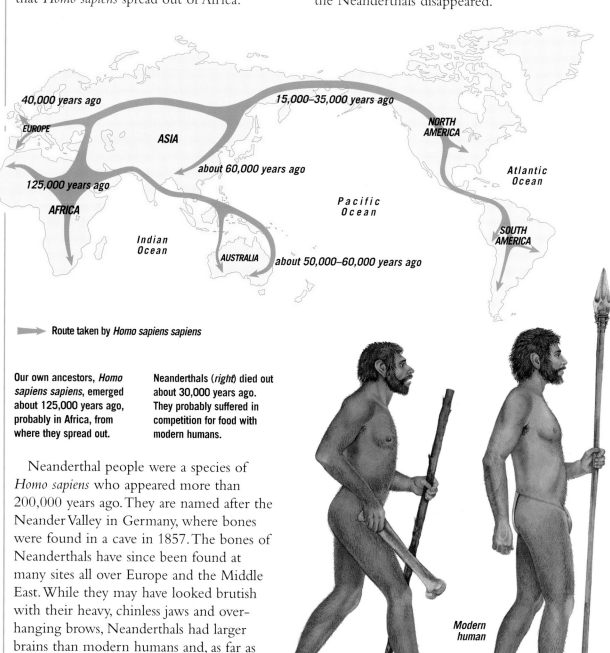

40,000 years ago

EUROPE

ASIA

15,000–35,000 years ago

NORTH AMERICA

about 60,000 years ago

Atlantic Ocean

125,000 years ago

AFRICA

Pacific Ocean

SOUTH AMERICA

Indian Ocean

AUSTRALIA about 50,000–60,000 years ago

Route taken by *Homo sapiens sapiens*

Our own ancestors, *Homo sapiens sapiens*, emerged about 125,000 years ago, probably in Africa, from where they spread out.

Neanderthals (*right*) died out about 30,000 years ago. They probably suffered in competition for food with modern humans.

Neanderthal people were a species of *Homo sapiens* who appeared more than 200,000 years ago. They are named after the Neander Valley in Germany, where bones were found in a cave in 1857. The bones of Neanderthals have since been found at many sites all over Europe and the Middle East. While they may have looked brutish with their heavy, chinless jaws and over-hanging brows, Neanderthals had larger brains than modern humans and, as far as we know, they were the first people to hold religious ceremonies and to bury their dead with possessions for the afterlife.

Modern human

Neanderthal

Humans began to paint and draw on cave walls thousands of years ago, long before they learned to write. The most famous examples of cave paintings were found at Lascaux in France in 1940 *(below)*. They were painted about 18,000 years ago using colors made from minerals in rocks. Sticks or bare hands were used to apply the color to the wall. The pictures, which were hidden away in dark parts of the cave, show animals the people hunted and are very realistic.

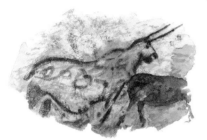

CAVE PAINTINGS

Life for early nomadic people consisted mainly of an endless hunt for food. Finds of cave paintings and other works of art show that some may have had religious beliefs and customs which they thought would help them in their quest for food. The cave paintings were not meant for display. They were painted or sometimes carved on dark walls and ceilings where no one could see them. The artists had to use burning branches to see by and climb ladders to reach their work. The animals are carefully painted using glowing colors.

People also left handprints by placing a hand on the wall and painting round it.

The fact that the paintings are hidden away suggests that they may have been part of a secret ritual to make the hunt more successful. The people may have believed that the pictures would help them to catch real animals. Or perhaps they thought that drawing the animals would ensure that they multiplied so that there were always plenty to hunt. Some of the pictures may have been straightforward records of the things the artists saw around them. Whatever the reasons for them, people went on painting and carving on cave walls for about 20,000 years and examples have been found in Europe, Africa, Asia, the Americas, and Australia. They give us many clues about changes in climate and environment.

HUNTER-GATHERERS

AS TIME WENT BY, hunters became more skilled and made more effective weapons. They were cunning and learned to use telltale signs for finding animals, such as footprints and broken branches. They also managed to trap some of the larger animals by driving them over cliffs or into bogs. As people developed language, they could communicate plans to one another, which also made hunting easier and more effective.

The Palaeolithic period, or Old Stone Age, describes the time between the first use of simple tools (which took place about 2.5 million years ago) to the start of the Neolithic period, or New Stone Age, when people began to farm the land and grow crops (12,000 years ago).

The hunters used spears, bows and arrows, and knives to kill prey, and fishhooks to catch fish from the rivers and lakes. They did not wander around aimlessly, hoping some animals would come their way. They studied the lie of the land and learned where animals were likely to gather or shelter. They also saw that some animals moved to different areas when the weather got colder or hotter. This study of their environment saved them a lot of time and effort and made life easier.

Most hunter-gatherers lived in small groups of two or three families because a woolly mammoth or a bison went a long way with fewer people to feed. Groups sometimes became larger if there was a lot of food around. Each group would probably have had a leader who made decisions and plans for the others.

About 20,000 years ago the world was in the grip of the Ice Age. Huge woolly mammoths abounded in northern regions. They were prey for the hunters.

Here, hunters are using wooden spears with sharp stone tips to catch their prey. Shaped pieces of wood or bone were used as spear-throwers, which helped the hunters throw their spears with more force. Fishermen trap fish from the lake in a net, while the women gather nuts and fruit.

The group did not stay in one place for long. Animals moved on and the hunters followed them.

GATHERING PLANTS

Hunting was important, but plant food was vital, too, because it provided a more varied diet. People came to know where certain nuts, fruit, and grasses grew. They learned that bees made honey, which could be used to sweeten food. They dug into the ground to find roots and tubers. Plants provided a regular supply of food during the growing season, which could keep the group nourished if hunting became difficult. But meat remained an essential part of the diet.

MAKING CLOTHES

Animal skins had many uses, including making clothes. First the skins had to be prepared so that they did not crack. Each skin was stretched out on the ground and scraped to remove the animal fat. Then it was smoothed with a bone tool to make it supple and easier to work with. When the skins were ready, they were cut into shape with a stone knife. Holes were punched along the edges so that they could be sewn together using a bone needle and a length of sinew (animal muscle tendon).

At the end of the day, the group gathers back at the camp. Shelters were made from whatever material was available. Some tents were made from animal skins draped over a simple wooden frame. Mammoth-hunters built igloo-shaped huts from mammoth bones. Shelters could also be made by weaving branches together to form a screen. This was curved around a frame of sticks to form a hut. It could be covered with skins to give extra warmth.

Huts or tents were often grouped in a circle to protect the people from wild animals and from bad weather. The fire also deterred the animals from coming any closer.

FIRST FARMERS

THE HUNTERS and gatherers of the late Palaeolithic period made other important advances. They tamed, or domesticated, wild animals such as wolves, which became the first hunting dogs. The people also realized that the seeds from grasses they picked could be sown in the ground to produce more plants.

Once these discoveries had been made, people could settle in permanent groups and form communities. The first farming communities began about 12,000 years ago. Farmers planted early forms of wheat and barley that grew wild on the hillsides, and domesticated animals such as sheep and goats for milk and meat.

The farmers needed sunshine and water for their crops. The first communities settled on the banks of rivers in the hot lands of the Middle East and North Africa. Some farmed the fertile soil on the banks of the Tigris and Euphrates rivers in Mesopotamia (modern-day Iraq: *see page 28*). Others settled in the valley of the River Nile in Egypt *(see page 16)*.

Groups of families built mud-brick houses clustered together to form villages. They learned to make the things they needed for farming: tools for working the land, baskets for gathering crops, and pots for storing food. The first farmers used very simple tools such as sticks, which they jabbed into the ground to make holes and shallow trenches for planting seeds.

PLOUGHING THE LAND

Farming was slow and laborious using these methods. Farmers could only grow enough food for themselves and their families, which meant that every able person in the community had to farm to survive.

Some new tools were needed to enable food to be produced more efficiently. One was the invention to the plough. The first plough was probably a bough with forked branches that could be pulled along the ground to turn the soil.

Most of our evidence about early ploughs comes from wall paintings and carvings. We know that a simple scratch plough was used in Mesopotamia from about 4500 B.C. and in ancient Egypt from about 2600 B.C.

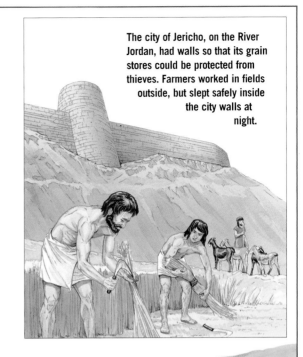

The city of Jericho, on the River Jordan, had walls so that its grain stores could be protected from thieves. Farmers worked in fields outside, but slept safely inside the city walls at night.

Early farmers in Mesopotamia use stone knives to harvest the wheat (1). The cut stalks are beaten with sticks to separate out the seeds (2). These are ground into flour for making bread (3).

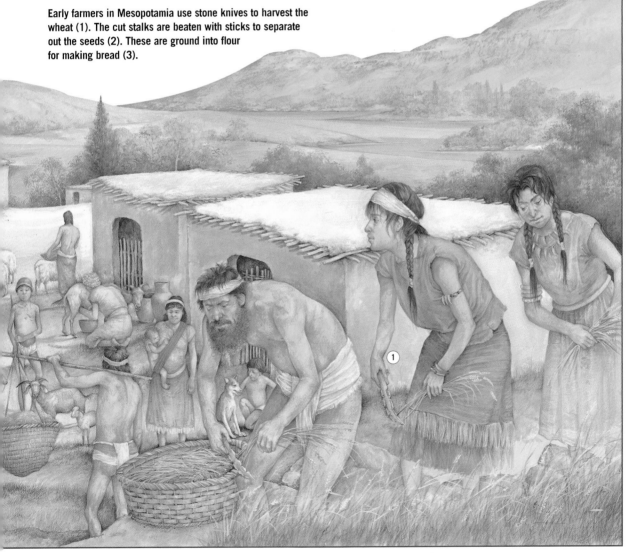

FIRST CITIES

EARLY VILLAGES were built of mud-brick which crumbled after a time. When the houses were no longer useable, new houses were built over the ruins. In time, a mound, called a *tell* in Arabic or *hüyük* in Turkish, formed as more buildings were built one top of the other.

Eventually towns and cities grew up on some of these sites. The ancient city of Çatal Hüyük *(below)* in Turkey had no outer wall to protect it. The houses were linked together and there were no streets. A ladder ran up to the roof of each house, where there was a door to get in. People moved around by crossing the rooftops. When the ladders were taken away, the city was safe.

Improved farming methods freed some people for other work. In Çatal Hüyük, craftspeople made products for trading, such as ornaments, jewelry, and cloth. Some craftspeople made mirrors by polishing a dark, glasslike mineral called obsidian.

The houses in Çatal Hüyük each had a living room, a storeroom, and a religious shrine. This illustration *(above)* shows what a shrine would have looked like. It contained plaster figures of the gods and sometimes wall paintings of animals.

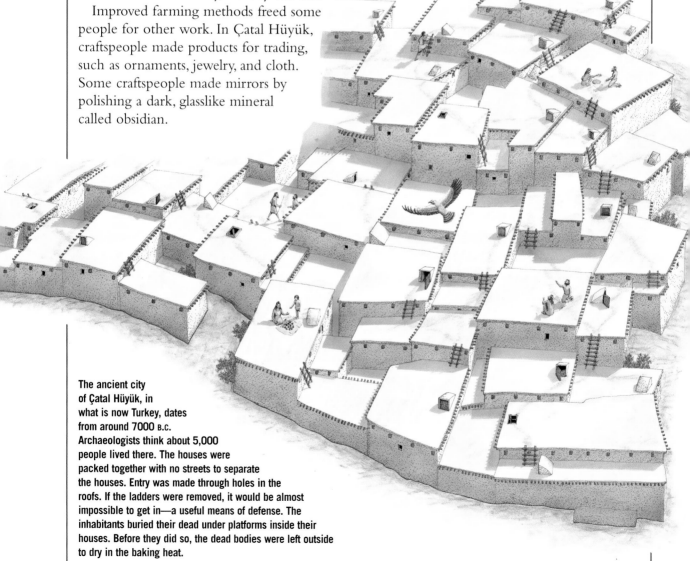

The ancient city of Çatal Hüyük, in what is now Turkey, dates from around 7000 B.C. Archaeologists think about 5,000 people lived there. The houses were packed together with no streets to separate the houses. Entry was made through holes in the roofs. If the ladders were removed, it would be almost impossible to get in—a useful means of defense. The inhabitants buried their dead under platforms inside their houses. Before they did so, the dead bodies were left outside to dry in the baking heat.

EARLY WRITING

WHEN PEOPLE BEGAN to trade with each other, it became essential to record the details in writing. Writing was invented by the ancient Sumerians in Mesopotamia about 5,500 years ago. The earliest writing was a series of marks scratched onto stone tablets. Later, scribes began to write on clay tablets using a reed pen called a stylus. The earliest writing was in picture form. This was very slow because there was a different picture for every word and scribes had to learn more than 2,000 symbols.

Early writing was slow and laborious and few people could write or read the symbols. For centuries, it was mainly used for recording taxes and details of ownership and sales. Later, people realized that words and syllables were made up of a few sounds and that each sound could be shown by a single letter. The first people to understand this were the Canaanites, who lived on the eastern shores of the Mediterranean. They developed an alphabet known as "Semitic" script. After this, different scripts began to follow. The Phoenicians *(see page 27)* used an alphabet which contained only consonants. The Greeks *(see page 32)* adopted it, introducing vowels as well. This was the beginning of the modern alphabet.

The word *alphabet* comes from "alpha" and "beta," the first two letters of the Greek alphabet. The Romans *(see page 38)* developed their alphabet (the one we still use today) from later versions of the Greek alphabet and some of the letters are similar.

The Chinese *(see page 25)* have never had an alphabet. Their writing consists of thousands of symbols or "characters."

Early writing in picture symbols on a clay tablet *(left)*. Symbols were later replaced by cuneiform. Below are two words written in both ways.

Bull   *Fish*

A scribe records the number of sheep and goats a farmer has. He is making symbols, called cuneiform, on a clay tablet, using a stylus with a wedge-shaped tip. This method was very slow and complex and mastered by only a few trained scribes. People had no way of recording numbers, so they counted on their fingers and thumbs.

The Mesopotamians gradually developed a method of writing using symbols. This was called "cuneiform" writing, from the Greek word for "wedge-shaped." The wedge-shaped tip of the stylus was used to make different symbols in soft clay. But even this system used about 600 symbols. Even so, cuneiform writing was adopted by the Assyrians, the Babylonians, and the Persians *(see pages 28–29)*.

Writing was invented for practical reasons but it is one of the major breakthroughs in history. In fact, history itself could not be recorded until people could write it down.

A society in which people live in towns, where many of them work as craftspeople, scribes, builders, merchants, and other occupations, is described as a civilized one. The first civilizations grew up in the Middle East, India, China, and Egypt.

ANCIENT EGYPT

ONE OF THE GREATEST and longest-lasting civilizations grew up on a narrow strip of fertile land along the banks of the River Nile in Egypt *(see map, right)*. The ancient Egyptians were surrounded by arid desert and their farming year relied on the annual flooding of the Nile. Yet their civilization lasted for 3,500 years and they created some of the most spectacular monuments of any in the ancient world.

The first Egyptians were wandering hunters who came from the desert to settle in the Nile Valley. They discovered that the summer floods provided fertile soil for growing grain and pasture for raising sheep, goats, and cattle. The Nile floods were essential but they could also be disastrous. If the waters rose at the wrong time of year, all the crops would be ruined. If there was not enough water, the crops would not grow and people would starve. Early Egyptian farmers learned to control the floodwaters by building dykes and ponds for storing water for use in time of drought.

As time passed, villages grew into towns and cities and the people developed a system of government. Craftspeople in the towns and cities learned to work metals such as copper. The potters' wheel, an import from Asia, was a valuable tool. Egypt became wealthy as trading increased.

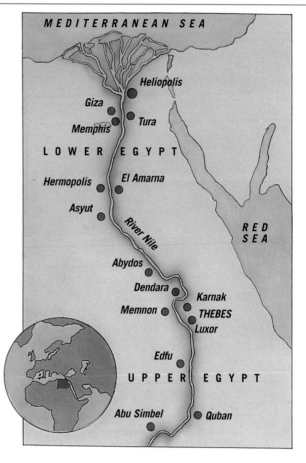

The pyramids were built as tombs for the pharaohs or kings of ancient Egypt. They were incredible feats of engineering for their time. Many survive today.

By about 3400 B.C. Egypt consisted of two kingdoms, Upper and Lower Egypt. In about 3100 B.C., Menes, a king of Nekhen in Upper Egypt conquered Lower Egypt and became the first pharaoh of both kingdoms. The history of Egypt is divided into three main periods: the Old Kingdom, the Middle Kingdom, and the New Kingdom.

At the time of the Old Kingdom (2575–2134 B.C.), belief in the afterlife became an important part of of ancient Egyptian religion. It was the age of pyramid-building *(see page 20)*. In the Middle Kingdom (2040–1640 B.C.), Egypt traded with other lands and conquered Nubia to the south.

The New Kingdom (1560–1070 B.C.) was Egypt's Golden Age. With their capital at Thebes, the pharaohs conquered lands in the Middle East and made their kingdom prosperous. The pharaohs built great temples. The wealth of ancient Egypt attracted other rulers. Egypt later fell to the armies of Assyria, Greece, Persia, and finally the Romans in 30 B.C.

This is a bust of of Queen Nefertiti (*left*), wife of Akhenaten (ruled 1379–1362 B.C.). They wanted to make the people abandon their many gods and instead worship only one, Aten, the sun in the sky. After their deaths, Egyptians reverted to their old ways. Queen Nefertiti ruled Egypt briefly in her own right.

Egypt was often in conflict with its neighbors and also with enemies from further afield. The pharaohs and their armies would ride out to conquer new lands and return home laden with riches taken in war. Most of the prisoners became slaves. The riches were used to embark on ambitious building projects, often in honor of the pharaohs' conquests. The two temples at Abu Simbel were built by Rameses II (ruled 1290–1224 B.C.) to commemorate his victory over the Hittites, who came from Syria. Outside the Great Temple are colossal seated statues of the king (*above, right*). The smaller temple is dedicated to Rameses' queen, Nefertari.

BOATS ON THE NILE

Boats on the Nile were the main form of transport in ancient Egypt. The earliest boats were made from bundles of papyrus (a reed that grows by the Nile) tied together. They had wooden paddles or long poles. Later boats were larger and had square sails. The boat in the picture has a large sail and two huge rudder oars for steering it.

From the evidence of models found in tombs, paintings and carvings, and the discovery of actual funeral boats, we have a good idea of what river craft looked like in ancient Egyptian times. This vessel dates from the New Kingdom period and was probably a royal or ceremonial ship.

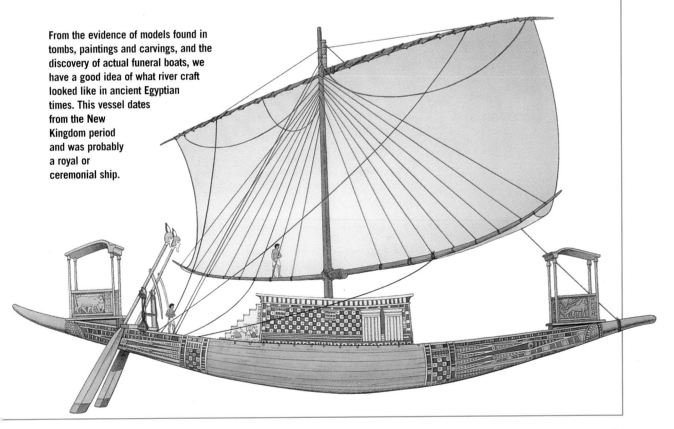

EVERYDAY LIFE

THE ANCIENT EGYPTIANS grew their crops in fertile black soil on the banks of the Nile. They learned to irrigate the land so that it was not too dry or too sodden after the floods. They dug channels between the fields to take water to fields that were further away from the river. They also invented a device called a *shaduf* for lifting water from the river to water the fields close by.

Most people were farmers, who worked throughout the year to provide food for people in the towns. Cattle pulled simple ploughs that turned the soil and prepared the fields for sowing the seeds.

Farmers grew wheat and barley, fruit and vegetables, and flax for making linen. The harvest was the most important time in the farming year, for if it was not successful, the people would starve. Before the crops were harvested, scribes wrote down the the size of the field and the amount of grain it would probably produce. Then the wheat or barley was cut down with sickles and made into sheaves, which were taken away for threshing (removing the ears of grain from the stalks). Cattle and donkeys were driven into the threshing enclosure to trample on the grain and separate it from the stalks. Then the grain was thrown into the air on shovels to clean it and separate out bits of straw and chaff.

KEY
1. A shaduf. *The weight helped to lift the bucket when it was full*
2. *Using a sickle to cut the crops*
3. *Making a sheaf*
4. *Loading the sheaves into baskets*
5. *Making bread*
6. *Fishing*

Harvest time in ancient Egypt. A harvester cuts the corn with a sickle while a helper ties bundles of stalks into sheaves. The sheaves are loaded onto donkeys and taken to the threshing enclosure. This could be in the field or near the farmhouse. The grain was ground into flour between millstones. Flour was used to make flat loaves of bread. On the river, fishermen are fishing with nets from a papyrus boat.

In Egyptian towns, people could obtain the things they needed from the markets. There was no money so people exchanged or bartered goods for others of similar value.

The scribes kept a strict eye on what the farmer produced because the crops did not really belong to the farmer. He was expected to hand most of them over to the government to feed people who were not farmers. If a farmer did not produce as much food as he should have, he was punished with a beating.

As food was produced more efficiently, larger numbers of people were able to do other types of work. Many of these people were craftspeople who had workshops in the towns. Often a son would learn his father's craft and follow him into the workshop.

The craftspeople were very skilled, despite only having simple tools to work with. There were stoneworkers, carpenters, potters, glassworkers, leatherworkers, spinners and weavers, metalworkers, and jewelers. The products they made were for trading with other countries as well as for the Egyptians themselves.

Egyptian houses were made of mud-brick and plastered white on the outside. Some had two stories. Windows were shuttered to keep the house cool. Inside the house, the walls were often exquisitely painted with bright designs.

Furniture was well designed and comfortable. Beds were made of wicker on a wooden frame and the sleepers rested their heads on wooden headrests. Couches had cushions stuffed with goose feathers, and tables and boxes were often decorated with inlaid designs.

Most Egyptians were farmers. Pharaohs and noblemen, however, enjoyed hunting dangerous prey— such as leopards and lions— for sport.

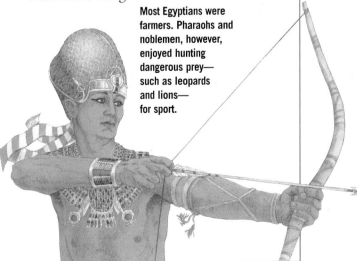

PYRAMIDS

THE BEST-KNOWN monuments of the ancient Egyptian civilization are the pyramids. They were built about 4,500 years ago, as huge tombs for the pharaohs of Egypt. The most famous pyramid site is at Giza, the only one of the Seven Wonders of the Ancient World to survive today. The site is made up of three large pyramids, the largest of which, the Great Pyramid, was 480 feet (147 m) high when first built.

The ancient Egyptians studied the movements of the stars, planets, and sun. They believed that the spirits of dead kings joined the gods among the stars. The pyramids were built to align with the Pole Star in the north, with each face pointing exactly north, south, east, and west. At the base of the pyramids, temples were built where priests would make offerings to the king's spirit. Small stone tombs were built around the pyramid for the king's family and courtiers.

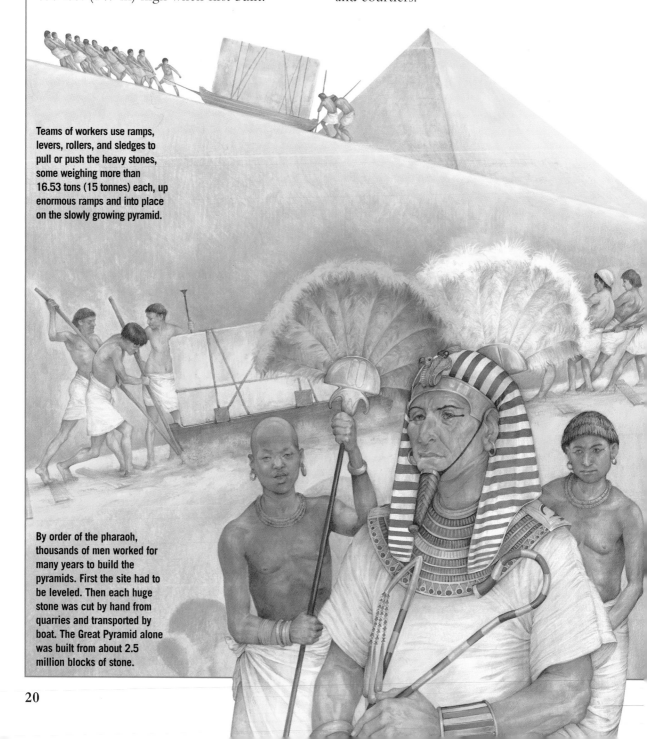

Teams of workers use ramps, levers, rollers, and sledges to pull or push the heavy stones, some weighing more than 16.53 tons (15 tonnes) each, up enormous ramps and into place on the slowly growing pyramid.

By order of the pharaoh, thousands of men worked for many years to build the pyramids. First the site had to be leveled. Then each huge stone was cut by hand from quarries and transported by boat. The Great Pyramid alone was built from about 2.5 million blocks of stone.

BURYING THE DEAD

Before a body could be placed inside the tomb, it had to be prepared for burial. All pharaohs and other very important people in Egypt were mummified, or preserved, after death. This was because the ancient Egyptians believed that only by preserving the body as a mummy could the spirit live on. People called embalmers were responsible for this process.

When the mummy had been completed, it was shut inside its brightly colored coffin. It was then placed into a heavy stone case, called a sarcophagus, in the burial chamber, along with treasures the pharaoh would need in the afterlife. The tomb was then sealed up as securely as possible. Unfortunately, robbers often broke into the

The case in which a mummy lay was painted with an image of the dead person, so that its spirit would recognize it in the afterlife. It was beautifully decorated with brightly colored paintings. Carefully painted hieroglyphics and scenes from the Book of the Dead, a book of magic spells, were meant to help the mummy on its journey to the afterlife.

As a result of the embalmer's skilled work, many bodies have not decayed thousands of years after mummification.

Many tombs and their treasures were plundered by thieves, but that of King Tutankhamun lay undisturbed in the Valley of the Kings for over 3,300 years. The tomb was finally discovered in 1922. Archaeologists were amazed to find it still full of treasure: gold, jewels, fine clothing, chariots, and musical instruments. A beautiful mask *(left)* made of gold and jewels covered the mummy's face. Tutankhamun was only about 17 years old when he died.

pyramids and stole the treasures in the burial chamber. Because of this, later pharaohs were buried not in pyramids but in tombs cut into the rocks of the secluded Valley of the Kings.

It was said that if a tomb was disturbed and the treasures taken, the mummies would be angry and would wreak terrible revenge. When Tutankhamun's tomb was discovered and emptied for scientific and historical examination, people feared that the dead pharaoh had put a curse on the people who had entered his tomb.

Embalmers had to make sure the body would not rot and decay after burial. First they removed all the inner organs (1), except the heart, placing them in special jars. Known as canopic jars, they were decorated with images of the heads of either the dead person or a god and were buried with the body. Next, the embalmers packed the body with salt, sand, and spices (2) and rubbed it with oils, wine, and resin, before wrapping it in layers of long linen bandages (3). The mummy was ready for burial.

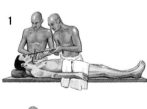

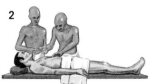

The mummified body was placed at the very deepest part of the pyramid, and the entrance was sealed with huge rocks. False passageways leading to empty rooms were also sealed, to confuse any would-be looters.

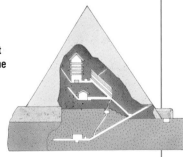

EDUCATION

ONLY THE PHARAOH'S children and the sons of wealthy families went to school. Girls stayed at home with their mothers, who taught them to look after the house, cook, spin, and weave. Farmers' children were also taught at home and were expected to go out to the fields from an early age, gathering crops and tending animals. Fishermen taught their children their own skills in the same way.

Many boys who received an education learned to be scribes. Scribes were highly regarded in ancient Egypt. It was the way to a good career. In the cities, classes were set up for scribes, where they were taught by officials such as priests or government administrators.

The would-be scribes had to learn to read and write in both hieroglyphic and hieratic scripts. Hieroglyphs, the oldest form of Egyptian writing, were picture symbols which could be used to make simple records or to write more complicated pieces such as poetry. But using hieroglyphs was a slow process because each picture symbol had to be painted separately. Hieratic script was a simplified form of hieroglyphic writing. It was more straightforward and quicker to use.

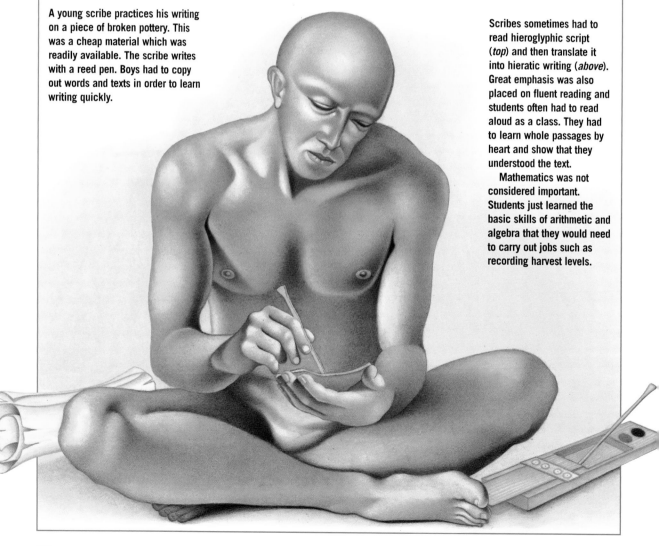

A young scribe practices his writing on a piece of broken pottery. This was a cheap material which was readily available. The scribe writes with a reed pen. Boys had to copy out words and texts in order to learn writing quickly.

Scribes sometimes had to read hieroglyphic script (*top*) and then translate it into hieratic writing (*above*). Great emphasis was also placed on fluent reading and students often had to read aloud as a class. They had to learn whole passages by heart and show that they understood the text.

Mathematics was not considered important. Students just learned the basic skills of arithmetic and algebra that they would need to carry out jobs such as recording harvest levels.

GODS AND TEMPLES

SOME scribes went to work in the temples, of which there were a great many in ancient Egypt. Temples had their own farms and workshops, libraries and "Houses of Life," which were offices where scribes wrote and copied religious documents and other texts for the temple. The priests were highly regarded and many held important government positions.

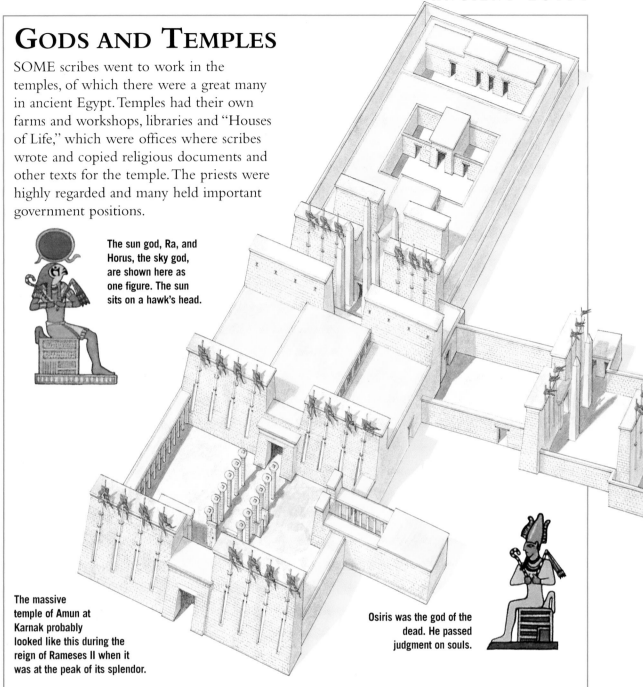

The sun god, Ra, and Horus, the sky god, are shown here as one figure. The sun sits on a hawk's head.

The massive temple of Amun at Karnak probably looked like this during the reign of Rameses II when it was at the peak of its splendor.

Osiris was the god of the dead. He passed judgment on souls.

The ancient Egyptians worshiped many different gods and their whole lives revolved around religion. Some of the gods were local and were only worshiped in certain towns or districts. Others were national gods who were worshiped in the major cities and the largest temples. These principal gods included Ra, the sun god; Ptah, the god of Memphis; Horus, the king's personal god; and Amun (Amon-Ra), a sun god and a god of the pharaohs, who was the most important of all the gods in Egypt.

The great temple to Amun at Karnak is one of Egypt's most amazing sights. It was built over many years and during the reigns of several pharaohs but was completed during the reign of Rameses II. The temple complex had ceremonial halls and avenues where processions took place, and thousands of servants and slaves worked there. Because so many people worshiped Amun, the priests at Karnak were some of the most powerful men in the land and were said to have a special relationship with the gods.

ANCIENT CHINA

THE CHINESE civilization grew up on the banks of the Huang (Yellow) River in northern China more than 7,000 years ago. It developed in isolation from the rest of the world for hundreds of years. Indeed, the Chinese people did not even realize that there were other civilized people in the world until the second century B.C. Until then, the only other people they came across were nomads from lands to the north and east.

Bones of *Homo erectus* have been found in China *(see page 7)*. The first settlers may have been descended from them, or from later groups of wandering *Homo sapiens*. Farmers cultivated crops in the deep, fertile soil on the riverbanks (the yellow soil that gave the river its name), and lived in small villages of huts made from mud and sticks. Farming methods became more efficient so farmers could produce enough food to feed people outside their own families. The population increased and began to spread to other parts of China.

A farming village on a plain in northern China in about 4500 B.C. At the center of the village is a pyramid-shaped hut where people can meet and talk. The farmers grew millet for making flour, and hemp which could be woven into a rough cloth.

As the Chinese civilization developed, ruling families, or dynasties, began to take power. The first such dynasty was the Shang which came to power in about 1750 B.C. By this time, there were some fairly large towns where people carried out different trades and crafts. Metalworkers used bronze, an alloy (mixture) of copper and tin, to make vessels for the king and noblemen. Bronze vessels found in Chinese burial grounds of this period have inscriptions on them, showing that the Shang had developed their own form of writing.

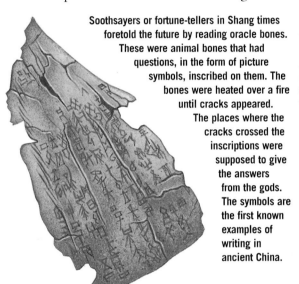

Soothsayers or fortune-tellers in Shang times foretold the future by reading oracle bones. These were animal bones that had questions, in the form of picture symbols, inscribed on them. The bones were heated over a fire until cracks appeared. The places where the cracks crossed the inscriptions were supposed to give the answers from the gods. The symbols are the first known examples of writing in ancient China.

A village in China in 1500 B.C. In the foreground the people are making bronze.

China was prosperous during the Shang dynasty. Ordinary people had to pay taxes to support the king and nobles. Craftspeople worked in many other materials besides bronze. They made wooden chariots for nobles and officials to ride around in, and ornaments in jade, a semiprecious stone.

The Shang dynasty was overthrown in about 1100 B.C. by a people from the valley of the River Wei, a tributary of the Huang River. They founded the Zhou dynasty which lasted for about 850 years. This was a time when Chinese scholars began to study philosophy, the meaning of life. The most important Chinese philosopher of the time was Confucius (551–479 B.C.).

The use of bronze meant that people could make strong tools and weapons in Shang China. Copper is a soft metal but when mixed with tin to make bronze, it becomes stronger. The Bronze Age had already begun in other lands, but the Chinese developed bronze independently. They made bronze weapons for hunting as well as warfare. Noblemen enjoyed hunting rhinoceros and tigers.

MINOAN CRETE

ONE OF THE GREATEST civilizations of the ancient world developed on the Greek island of Crete. Little was known about it until the British archaeologist Sir Arthur Evans (1851–1941) began digging on Crete in 1900 and uncovered the remains of a magnificent palace at Knossos. Four other palaces were also found on the island. Evans and other archaeologists found many treasures, including wall paintings and clay tablets which told them about the lifestyle of the people who had lived there. But there was a missing link. Nowhere could they find the name of this mysterious civilization. So they decided to call the people Minoans after their legendary ruler King Minos, who, according to Greek legend, ruled like a tyrant from Knossos.

The Minoans arrived on Crete in about 6000 B.C. and had begun to build their palaces by 2000 B.C. They made their wealth by trading around the Mediterranean. Large towns built up around the palaces *(below)*. Knossos was the largest

The dangerous sport of bull-leaping was played by athletic young men and women, who grasped the bull's horns and somersaulted over its back.

of these and, at its peak, probably had a population of about 100,000 people. Many were craftspeople who produced exquisite pottery, jewelry, and metalwork. Minoan nobles lived in country villas as well as in the towns, and seem to have enjoyed a luxurious lifestyle. There is no evidence of any wars or unrest on the island and the Minoans probably led peaceful lives.

What happened to the Minoans? They vanished in about 1450 B.C., possibly following the eruption of the nearby volcanic island of Thera, which spread huge volumes of volcanic ash over Crete.

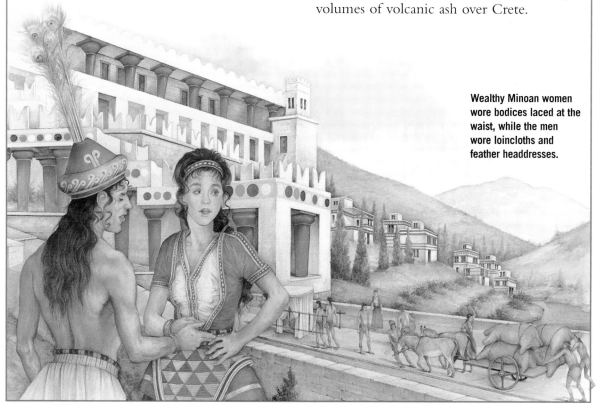

Wealthy Minoan women wore bodices laced at the waist, while the men wore loincloths and feather headdresses.

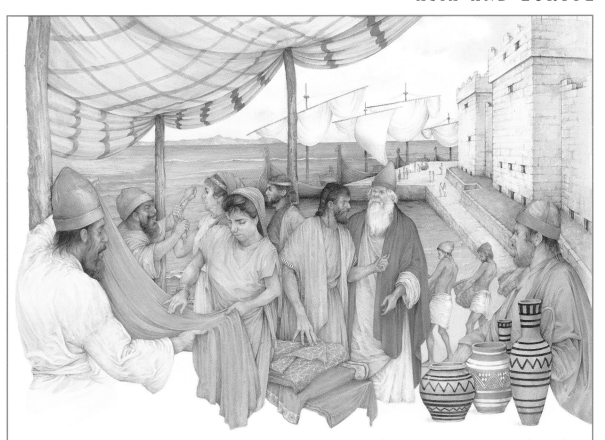

THE PHOENICIANS

LIKE THE MINOANS, the Phoenicians were Mediterranean traders, active between the years 1500 and 1000 B.C. They lived along the eastern shores of the Mediterranean Sea. At first they were known as Canaanites, but later went under the name of Phoenicians, from the Greek word *phoinos,* which means red, the color of a dye they traded. The Phoenicians were skillful and daring sailors for their time. They built fast warships to escort their merchant ships on trading voyages. These ships had a square sail and two banks of oarsmen. Examples of their ivory carvings, glassware, jewelry, and metalwork have been found all over the Mediterranean lands. As well as exporting goods, they sailed off in search of raw materials, such as metals, even traveling around the west coast of Africa.

The Phoenicians dominated the Mediterranean during the first millennium B.C. In 814 B.C. they founded Carthage, a city in what is now Tunisia, which quickly expanded into a powerful state.

Many Phoenician exports came from the natural resources of their land. Cedars and pine trees grew in the mountains and these could be exported to lands such as Egypt, where wood was scarce. The trees also provided precious oils for export. The Phoenicians made glass from sand and wove fine wool and linen, which they dyed with a purple dye made from a local type of sea snail. This famous Tyrian cloth, named after their city of Tyre, was one of the most popular of Phoenician exports *(above)*.

The Phoenicians also developed an alphabet which merchants used for trading. The Canaanite script, as it was called, was adopted by the Greeks and formed the basis of our modern alphabet *(see page 15)*.

The Etruscan civilization emerged in central Italy in about 800 B.C. Known for their art and architecture, the Etruscans had links with both Greece *(see page 32)* and Carthage. Music *(right)* was an important part of their culture.

MESOPOTAMIA

MESOPOTAMIA, the fertile land between the Tigris and Euphrates rivers in what is now Iraq, was one of the first places to be settled when people decided to form communities *(see page 12)*. The Sumerians, who first formed a civilization there, were conquered in about 2370 B.C. Different groups of invaders then founded new city-states, which struggled to rule the area for the next 500 years. Then Hammurabi came to the throne of one of the city-states, Babylon, in 1792 B.C. He brought other city-states under his control. Babylon dominated Mesopotamia.

Hammurabi was a wise king who set out a new code of laws. These gave status to women, protected poor people, and punished wrongdoers. Unlike previous rulers, Hammurabi did not regard himself as a god. During his reign, Babylon was a rich city, the capital of a kingdom known as Babylonia. Massive stepped pyramid temples, called ziggurats, were built to worship the gods. The most famous of these was the Tower of Babel. It was, the Bible says, designed to reach Heaven.

Six centuries after Hammurabi's death in 1750 B.C., the kingdom he founded was eventually conquered by a warlike people, the Assyrians.

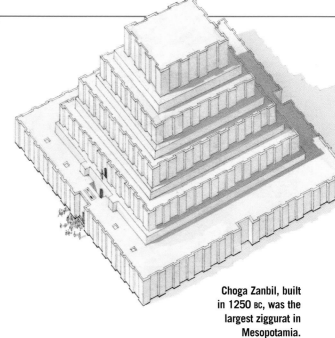

Choga Zanbil, built in 1250 BC, was the largest ziggurat in Mesopotamia.

THE ASSYRIANS

The land of the Assyrians, in northern Mesopotamia, lay on important trade routes. They wanted to dominate the area by building up a great empire. Many years of warfare followed, during which the Assyrian empire expanded to cover most of the Near East. The ruler during the main period of expansion was Assurbanipal the last great Assyrian king. Archaeologists found 20,000 clay tablets in his library at the palace of Nineveh. These give many details about Assyrian laws and history.

One of the features of Assyrian life was the royal lion hunt, when the king and his party went out to destroy the mountain lions which preyed on people and animals. Assyrian artists made fine carvings of such events.

NEBUCHADNEZZAR

Babylon became powerful again during the reign of King Nabopolassar (ruled 625–605 B.C.), who managed to overthrow the Assyrians and win back the city's power. His son, Nebuchadnezzar II (ruled 605–562 B.C.) fought the Egyptians and conquered Assyria and Judah. He built many fine ziggurats and palaces and created the Hanging Gardens of Babylon, one of the Seven Wonders of the Ancient World.

The Babylonians were keen astronomers. They studied the stars and planets and tried to work out their positions in relation to the earth. They believed that the earth was a flat disc suspended in space on a cushion of air. Some scientists of ancient Greece also adopted this theory.

Babylonian mathematicians were the first to divide a day into 24 hours, each hour into 60 minutes, and each minute into 60 seconds. These ancient units of time have, of course, survived to this day.

Babylonian scientists study the stars.

Nebuchadnezzar made Babylon the finest city of its day. The Greek historian Herodotus described it as "surpassing in splendor any city of the known world." Archaeologists excavating Babylon at the beginning of the 20th century found that the city wall made a circle almost 11 miles (18 km) long. (Unfortunately, they found no trace of the Hanging Gardens.) The Babylonians built in mud-brick covered with glazed tiles, on which artists created sculptured designs.

Babylon had eight gateways in its walls, the finest of which was the Ishtar Gate. Built to honor the goddess of love and battle, the gateway, through which sacred processions would have passed, was 30 feet (15 m) high. The walls surrounding it were covered in glazed blue bricks, decorated with carvings of dragons and bulls.

The dragons shown on the walls of the Ishtar Gate were symbols of the Babylonians' chief god, Marduk. The bulls represented the lightning god, Adad. The gate was at the northern entrance to the city of Babylon. It has been completely reconstructed and now stands in a museum in Berlin, Germany.

EUROPE IN THE BRONZE AGE

THE FIRST METAL objects in Europe were produced from copper or gold and date from about 5000 B.C. These metals, easy to shape into jewelry and other artifacts, were too soft for making tools and weapons. The discovery around 2300 B.C. that copper could be strengthened by mixing, or alloying, it with another metal, tin, heralded the start of the Bronze Age in Europe. By about 1200 B.C., metalworkers in Europe had switched almost entirely to using bronze.

At this time, people in Europe had not formed great civilizations in the same way that some peoples in other parts of the world had. They lived in simple farming communities *(below)*. A patch of forest was cleared by cutting down and burning trees. Then the people built huts of mud and straw and grew crops such as wheat.

By about 1500 B.C. communities had become more complex. The leaders of the communities were not gods or remote nobles like the kings in other parts of the ancient world, but farmers or craftpeople, just like the people themselves. However, these leaders, or chieftains, wanted recognition of their rank in life. They liked to wear luxurious clothes adorned with gold and carry expensive bronze weapons signifying their prowess as a warrior. When a chieftain died, these treasures were put in his tomb to serve him in the next world.

Some early European metalworking communities lived in forts. The chieftain lived near the center of the settlement, which was surrounded by wooden palisades (high fences) and ditches to give him protection against invading enemies. By 1250 B.C., bronze swords and helmets were in use. The metalworkers were so important that their workshops were often packed closely together inside the fort, while the farmers lived in simple huts outside.

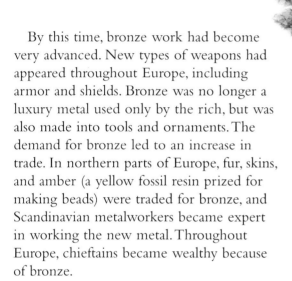

A farming community in 1500 B.C. The farmers have simple ploughs to work the land, and oxen to pull them. Here the farmer ploughs the land before sowing wheat. The people can produce everything they need in the village. They chop wood for their fires and spin yarn and weave cloth to make clothes. If they can grow enough food, they can exchange it for other products such as metal.

By this time, bronze work had become very advanced. New types of weapons had appeared throughout Europe, including armor and shields. Bronze was no longer a luxury metal used only by the rich, but was also made into tools and ornaments. The demand for bronze led to an increase in trade. In northern parts of Europe, fur, skins, and amber (a yellow fossil resin prized for making beads) were traded for bronze, and Scandinavian metalworkers became expert in working the new metal. Throughout Europe, chieftains became wealthy because of bronze.

STONE MONUMENTS

By about 2000 B.C. people in Europe had begun to build huge stone monuments for religious worship. To build Stonehenge (*below*), which stands on Salisbury Plain in southern England, massive stones had to be dragged across the plain on rollers, placed in deep pits, and then hauled upright.

ANCIENT GREECE

THE HISTORY of ancient Greece begins with the Mycenaeans, a warlike people who created a powerful and wealthy civilization in about 1550 B.C.

The first settlers in Greece lived in simple stone houses and farmed the land. These people, who later came to be called the Mycenaeans, began to trade around the Mediterranean and came into contact with the Minoan civilization on Crete *(see page 26)*. They borrowed many ideas and skills from the Minoans and began to make superb craftwork of their own.

The Mycenaeans were very different from the Minoans, however. The Minoans were a peaceful race, but the Mycenaeans were warriors. Their palaces were surrounded by massive walls. Inside, former rulers were buried in large, beehive-shaped tombs, called *tholoi*. From their palace strongholds, the Mycenaeans set off on raids around the Mediterranean.

Four gold death masks of kings were found in the royal tombs at Mycenae. This one was once thought to be the mask of Agamemnon, a king of Mycenae at the time of the Trojan War. Experts now think it is 300 years older, so could not be his.

Legends about the Mycenaeans date back thousands of years. One, told in the *Iliad* by the Greek poet Homer, gives an account of the war between Greece and Troy. The Mycenaean king, Agamemnon, set out to rescue his brother's beautiful wife Helen, who had been captured by the Trojan prince, Paris. After 10 years of fighting, Agamemnon's army finally defeated Troy by trickery. Greek soldiers hid inside a wooden horse *(below)*, which was towed into the city by the triumphant Trojans, thinking the Greeks had gone home. At nightfall, the Greeks emerged to capture the city.

GREEK WARFARE

City-states consisted of a main city or town and the villages around it. Each one was ruled by powerful nobles. Sometimes the nobles were overthrown by a tyrant, someone who took power although he had no right to do so.

By about 500 B.C., each city-state had its own army. One of the most formidable came from the city-state of Sparta in the south. By this time, the Classical Age (see page 34) had begun in Greece and the city-state of Athens was a haven for thinkers and artists. To the Spartans, however, the important thing was to make war.

Most of the Greek armies were made up of young men who trained as soldiers for two years after they left school. They were called up to join the army if there was a war (when they were known as conscripts). The Spartans, however, had a full-time army who were always ready to fight.

All Greek armies fought in a phalanx formation. The soldiers formed closely packed rows so that their shields partly protected their neighbor. Then they advanced on the enemy like a battering ram. The first few rows held their spears out in front of them so they could strike the enemy from a distance. The close formation made them difficult targets, so the phalanx was a very effective way of fighting.

A foot soldier from the Greek city-state of Sparta was called a hoplite. He wore armor over a short pleated tunic. Hoplites carried a shield and fought with a spear or a sword.

The Mycenaean civilization disappeared around 1200 B.C. Afterward, there was a period known as the Dark Ages until about 800 B.C., when the Greek civilization began to develop. Greece was not one country but a group of separate city-states. City-states fought each other to gain more power.

The Greeks had fleets of warships called triremes. Although it had square linen sails so that it could take advantage of the wind, a trireme was rowed into battle. The ship was rowed by three rows of oarsmen, one above the other. The rowers at the bottom level were inside the ship and their oars came out through portholes. On the front of the ship was a battering ram for ramming holes in enemy ships.

LIFE IN ATHENS

THE CLASSICAL AGE was a time when Greece flowered in the arts, philosophy, and science. The city-state of Athens was at its most powerful during this period. The city had been destroyed by the Persians in 480 B.C., but it was rebuilt in great splendor. One of the most magnificent projects of all was the group of buildings on the Acropolis, a rock that still dominates Athens today. At the heart of the Acropolis buildings was the Parthenon, a marble temple dedicated to the city's goddess, Athena.

Much of what we know about the ancient Greeks comes from the arts and literature of the time. Pottery was often decorated with scenes from everyday life. Sculptors created beautiful statues, philosophers wrote down their thoughts and ideas, and dramatists created plays based on real-life events.

The ancient Greeks worshiped many gods and goddesses. The 12 most important gods were said to live on Mount Olympus, the highest mountain in Greece. Zeus was the chief of the Olympian gods.

Greek athletes practiced for the sports festival held every four years at Olympia in southern Greece. This festival was the forerunner of the Olympic Games which are still held today.

Modern theater had its roots in ancient Greece. The audience sat on stone seats in the semicircular, open-air auditorium. The actors wore large comedy or tragedy masks so that the audience could see them. These masks are still the symbol of the theater today.

Every large city had a theater and drama was popular entertainment. The earliest form of theater was a festival of songs and dances. Later, playwrights such as Sophocles and Aristophanes began to write plays which actors could perform. There were two main types, comedies and tragedies. Many of these plays, written centuries ago, are still famous today.

Plays were performed on 10 days of each year. Audiences went to the theater for the whole day. They would usually see three tragedies or three comedies and a short play called a satire, which poked fun at a serious legend or event.

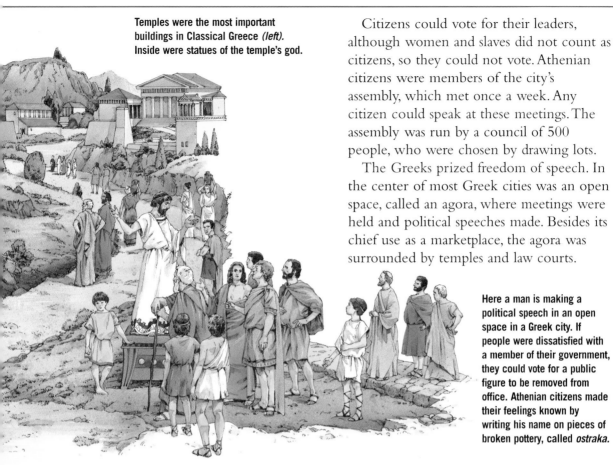

Temples were the most important buildings in Classical Greece *(left)*. Inside were statues of the temple's god.

Citizens could vote for their leaders, although women and slaves did not count as citizens, so they could not vote. Athenian citizens were members of the city's assembly, which met once a week. Any citizen could speak at these meetings. The assembly was run by a council of 500 people, who were chosen by drawing lots.

The Greeks prized freedom of speech. In the center of most Greek cities was an open space, called an agora, where meetings were held and political speeches made. Besides its chief use as a marketplace, the agora was surrounded by temples and law courts.

Here a man is making a political speech in an open space in a Greek city. If people were dissatisfied with a member of their government, they could vote for a public figure to be removed from office. Athenian citizens made their feelings known by writing his name on pieces of broken pottery, called *ostraka*.

In ancient Greece, people spoke out against being ruled by rich citizens and of having no say in how they were ruled. A new system of government, called *demokratia,* which means "government by the people," was introduced in Athens. Our English word "democracy" comes from this word. In Greek democracies, all citizens had a say in how the city-state was run, much as people have a say in democracies today.

MEDICINE

The basis of modern medicine also comes from ancient Greece. During the Classical Age, a man called Hippocrates founded a school of medicine on the Greek island of Kos, where diagnosis of illness was based on examination of patients. Doctors had to take the Hippocratic oath, which outlined their duties and responsibilities. Doctors still have to take this oath today.

The ruins of the Acropolis temples can still be seen in Athens today. The Greeks used columns like the ones supporting the Parthenon for many of their temples and public buildings. Columns were made by standing one block of stone on top of another. The top of the column was usually decorated with carvings.

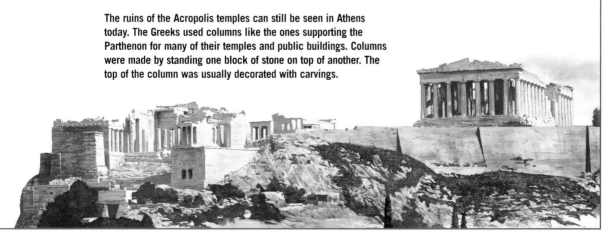

ALEXANDER THE GREAT

ALEXANDER the Great came from Macedonia, a wild mountainous area on the northern borders of Greece. His father, Philip, became king of Macedonia in 359 B.C. and united all of Greece under his rule. When he died in 336 B.C., Alexander became the new king at the age of 20.

Alexander had been taught by the Greek writer and philosopher Aristotle and this gave him a love of Greek poetry and art. But he was also a brave and brilliant soldier and his main interest was in building up a mighty empire for Greece.

Alexander's first battle was with the Greeks' old enemy, the Persians. In 334 B.C. he marched into Asia and defeated Darius III, the king of Persia, and his army. Alexander now set out to bring the whole of the Persian empire under Greek rule. His next move was to capture the Phoenician town of Tyre and then to defeat Egypt. He went on to capture the three palaces of the Persian kings at Babylon, Susa, and Persepolis. He spent three years vanquishing the eastern part of the Persian empire, then marched on to conquer the northern part of India in 326.

By now, Alexander and his army had been on the march for 11 years. He wanted to go further into India but his soldiers were tired of fighting and wanted to return home. Alexander agreed to turn back but died of a fever in Babylon in 323 B.C. He was only 32 years old.

Alexander was a fearless leader with a desire to conquer new lands. He set out with an army of 30,000 foot soldiers and 5,000 cavalry. He fought for 11 years to expand the Greek empire.

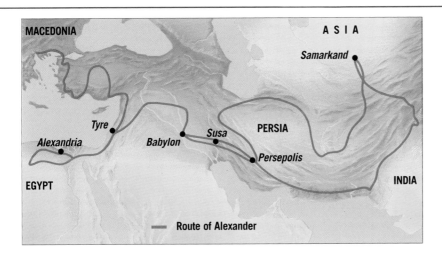

Alexander the Great formed an empire that consisted of a good part of the world then known to the Greeks. His travels took him down through the Near East and into Egypt, then across Asia and into northern India. To Alexander, India marked the end of the known world and he wanted to go on, but his soldiers refused. His horse, Bucephalus, which had carried him on his march, was killed in the battle against the Indian king, Poros, in 326 B.C.

As Alexander defeated more lands, he formed Greek colonies to stop the newly conquered peoples rebelling. The colonies, 16 of which were cities called Alexandria, were governed by his own soldiers. But Alexander died without a final plan for his massive empire. The lands were eventually divided into three parts, Macedonia, Persia, and Egypt, with a Greek general in charge of each. The period between Alexander's death and the defeat of the Greek empire by the Romans in 30 B.C. is known as the Hellenistic period.

The Hellenistic period was an age of scientific discovery, and the city of Alexandria in Egypt was its main center of learning. Many poets and scholars came to study at Alexandria. The mathematicians Pythagoras and Euclid worked out their rules in geometry there, while other scholars studied medicine and the movement of the stars.

The city of Petra in Jordan was inhabited by a people called the Nabateans. They were greatly influenced by Hellenistic architecture.

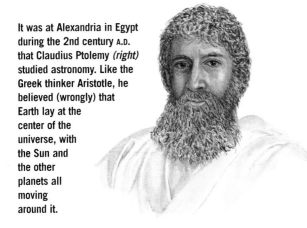

It was at Alexandria in Egypt during the 2nd century A.D. that Claudius Ptolemy (right) studied astronomy. Like the Greek thinker Aristotle, he believed (wrongly) that Earth lay at the center of the universe, with the Sun and the other planets all moving around it.

With no single leader, Alexander's empire was vulnerable to attack and was gradually taken over by the Romans. Egypt, the seat of learning, survived for longer than the rest of the empire, but the Roman emperor Augustus conquered it in 30 B.C. The queen was Cleopatra, the last of the Ptolemy family to rule in Egypt. She killed herself with her Roman lover, Mark Antony.

The legacy of Greece was revived during the Renaissance, or "rebirth," of thought and art in 15th-century Europe, and has influenced people ever since.

THE ROMANS

THE ROMANS came from the part of Europe we now call Italy. They built up an empire that was even larger than that of Alexander the Great *(see page 36)*.

Groups of people from northern Asia began to settle in Italy between 2000 and 1000 B.C. One group, which spoke a language called Latin, settled on the banks of the River Tiber. In time, this settlement became the city of Rome.

The Romans had several kings but the people were not happy with the way they were treated. They decided to set up a republic with a leader who was chosen by the people for a set length of time. If they did not like the way the leader did things, they could choose another leader at the end of that time.

Rome was a republic for nearly 500 years, during which time the Roman army conquered many new lands. But in 27 B.C., after the Roman defeat of Egypt and the deaths of Antony and Cleopatra *(see page 35)*, a dictator once again took control. This was Augustus, the first Roman emperor. By this time the Roman Empire had a population of 60 million people.

Britain was one of the Romans' conquests. Queen Boudicca and her tribe, the Iceni, rebelled against the Romans and recaptured many of their towns in Britain before she was defeated.

Roman foot soldiers were known as legionaries. A legionary wore an iron helmet and armor over a woollen tunic and a leather kilt. He had to carry his sword, a dagger, a shield, a spear, and all his provisions.

The first Roman army was made up of ordinary citizens, but at the height of the empire the soldiers were highly trained professionals. The army was divided into legions of about 6,000 foot soldiers or legionaries. A legion consisted of 10 cohorts each of which had six centuries, or companies of 100 men. A group of 700 cavalry rode on horses with each legion.

A Roman soldier was trained to carry all his own equipment, which consisted of clothes, a tent, food and cooking pots as well as his armor and weapons. The army often marched 20 miles (30 km) a day. Nothing stood in their way. If they came to a deep river they built a floating bridge by tying rafts of wood together.

THE GOVERNMENT

When Rome became a republic the people were determined that no one should have too much power, so they elected officials, known as magistrates, who governed the land. The most powerful magistrates were the two consuls who were elected to serve for one year and were expected to govern Rome in agreement with each other. After a year, most magistrates became members of the senate, who advised new officials.

Julius Caesar was a brilliant general who conquered many lands for Rome. He was elected consul in 59 B.C., but it was not long before he wanted to govern Rome in his own way. He became governor of parts of southern Gaul (now France) and brought northern Gaul under Roman rule. He returned to Rome in triumph and began to rule it as a dictator (someone who has absolute power) in 46 B.C. But some senators were jealous of Caesar and wanted to regain power for the senate. In 44 B.C. a group of senators stabbed him to death in the senate house in Rome.

After Caesar's death, two prominent Romans began to struggle for power. One was a fellow consul of Caesar's, Mark Antony, who became the lover of Cleopatra, queen of Egypt. The other was Caesar's great-nephew, Octavian. Octavian declared war on Antony and Cleopatra in 31 B.C. and defeated them at the Battle of Actium. Antony and Cleopatra killed themselves. Octavian became the first emperor of Rome, called Augustus, in 27 B.C.

Emperors ruled over the Roman Empire for over 400 years. They were not kings but they had absolute power over their people. The emperor's "crown" was a laurel wreath, a sign of military success.

The first emperor, Augustus, reigned from 27 B.C. to A.D. 14. He brought peace to the empire, but before his death he chose his own successor. From then on, the Romans could not choose their leader.

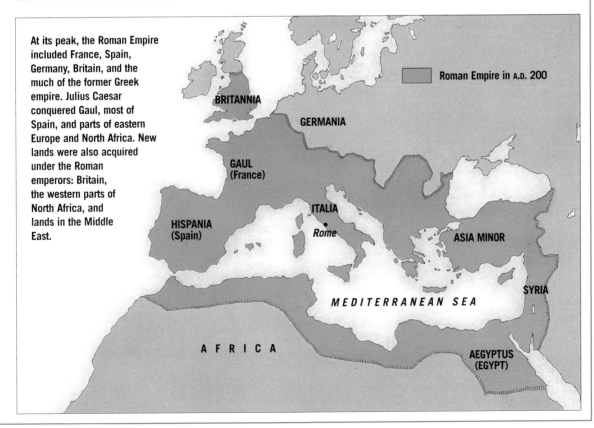

At its peak, the Roman Empire included France, Spain, Germany, Britain, and the much of the former Greek empire. Julius Caesar conquered Gaul, most of Spain, and parts of eastern Europe and North Africa. New lands were also acquired under the Roman emperors: Britain, the western parts of North Africa, and lands in the Middle East.

Roman Empire in A.D. 200

BRITANNIA

GERMANIA

GAUL (France)

ITALIA
Rome

HISPANIA (Spain)

ASIA MINOR

SYRIA

MEDITERRANEAN SEA

AFRICA

AEGYPTUS (EGYPT)

TOWN LIFE

AS THE ROMANS conquered new lands and built up their empire, they introduced their own lifestyle to the conquered peoples. Many signs of Roman habitation can still be seen today.

The Romans adopted many ideas from the Greeks, but their civilization had many distinctive aspects of its own. The Romans were excellent engineers and builders—and they liked their home comforts.

Archaeologists have found examples of Roman towns throughout the empire. The first Roman houses were built of brick or stone but the Romans also used what seems a very modern material, concrete. Some later Roman houses were built of concrete decorated with brick or stone.

The streets in the towns were laid out on a grid system, which means that they were straight and crossed one another at right angles. Many of the towns were first built as forts for the soldiers. Others were built for Roman citizens who decided to settle in the conquered lands. Roman settlers brought seeds from Italy to plant and grow their own food. Today, some fruit and vegetables which originally came from Italy have become native to the lands they were taken to by the Romans.

Farmers from the countryside brought their produce into the towns to sell in the market. The forum was the main market-place as well as the center of government. The Romans used coins; people bought things for a set price rather than barter and exchange of goods.

A Roman town in France. The local way of life and the style of buildings are Roman.

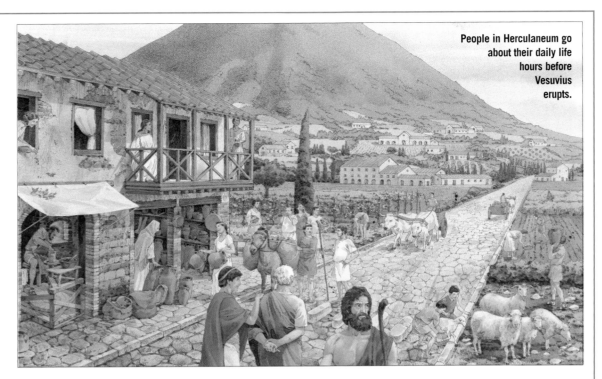

People in Herculaneum go about their daily life hours before Vesuvius erupts.

Much of our evidence about Roman houses and towns comes from the ruins of two cities, Pompeii and Herculaneum, which were destroyed in A.D. 79, when the volcano Vesuvius erupted. Pompeii was buried under hot ash, while Herculaneum disappeared under mud washed down from the volcano. Thousands of people were killed. Whole streets of shops and houses have been excavated in both cities.

Wealthy Romans lived in spacious villas with several rooms. At the center of the villa was the atrium, the main hall, which had an open roof to let in light. A pool called an *impluvium* caught rainwater that came in through the open roof. The rooms of the villa were arranged around the atrium.

Poor people's homes were very different. Some people lived in flats above shops, or in houses divided into rooms or flats.

People who lived in town houses enjoyed a life of luxury. Much information about the furniture in the houses comes from wall paintings at Pompeii. People lay on couches to eat their meals, which were laid out on low tables by slaves. Clothes, food, and books were stored in wooden cupboards and chests. Women and honored guests could sit on chairs, but everyone else sat on stools. Besides these, there was little furniture. As well as bedrooms and living rooms, houses had libraries. The inhabitants of the house could stroll in a courtyard, or worship at the shrine of the household god.

ROMAN BUILDERS

THE ROMANS were skilful builders and engineers. They built over 52,000 miles (85,000 km) of roads throughout their empire and many aqueducts to carry water from rivers or lakes to the towns, some of them huge stone structures built across valleys.

Roman roads were planned by surveyors who traveled with the army. The roads were planned to take the shortest route and to be as straight as possible. When the route had been decided, soldiers and slaves dug a wide trench. The road was then built by packing layers of stone, sand, and concrete into the trench.

Building an aqueduct and a road in a valley during Roman times.

AT THE BATHS

Wealthy Romans had baths and central heating in their houses. The heating was provided by the hypocaust (heating system) below ground, which passed hot air through channels in the walls.

Most towns had public baths that anyone could visit. Besides a way of keeping clean and healthy, it was an opportunity to meet friends and make conversation. The baths had several rooms and bathers passed through each one. In the main room, the *caldarium*, a slave rubbed oil into the bather's body. The bather soaked in a large warm bath, then went into a room where a basin of very hot water filled the air with steam (the *sudatorium*, after the Latin word *sudor*, meaning sweat). The bather scraped off the oil and dirt with a device called a strigil. Bathers coming from the *caldarium* went next into the *tepidarium*, to cool off a little before entering the *frigidarium*, where there was a cold bath to plunge into. This closed the pores of the skin.

In between the various stages of bathing, people sat and chatted or enjoyed a swim in the large, warm bath. People also did some vigorous exercise, such as going to the gym (the *sphaeristerium*), before visiting the baths.

The Romans built public baths in towns throughout their empire. Some of these can still be seen today. The water in the Great Bath at Bath, England, still flows along the channels made by the Romans.

Men went to the baths after work. Women could only use them at certain times.

The water for baths and all other purposes was brought along aqueducts. The word aqueduct comes from the Latin words for "water" and "to draw along." The aqueduct was a channel for carrying clean water from rivers and lakes to the towns, usually at ground level or through underground pipes. Aqueducts across valleys were built up on arches. About 200 Roman aqueducts can still be seen throughout the former empire.

The Roman aqueduct of Pont du Gard, near Nîmes in France, as it looks today, nearly 2,000 years after it was built. The Romans looked for a river or lake that was slightly higher than the town it was supplying. Then they built the aqueduct so that it sloped gradually downhill toward the town. The rows of arches across valleys had to keep the same slope as the rest of the channel.

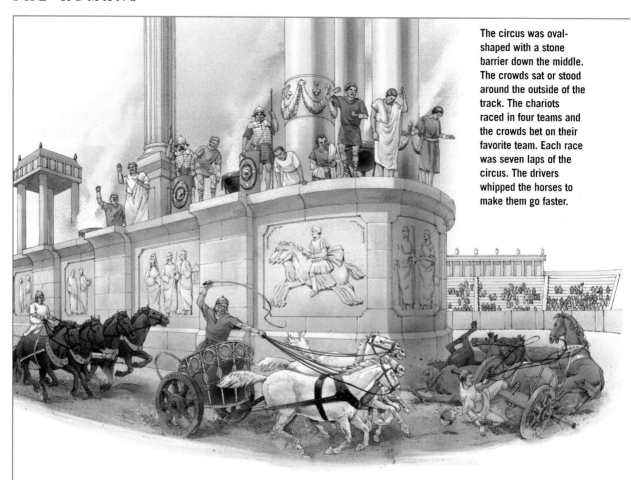

The circus was oval-shaped with a stone barrier down the middle. The crowds sat or stood around the outside of the track. The chariots raced in four teams and the crowds bet on their favorite team. Each race was seven laps of the circus. The drivers whipped the horses to make them go faster.

SPORTS

THE ROMANS had about 120 public holidays each year. On these days, Roman citizens went out to celebrate by going to the theater, or watching a chariot race or a fight between gladiators.

Chariot races and gladiator fights were held in the town's circus, which was a large, oval-shaped arena.

Chariot races were very dangerous. The drivers raced their horse-drawn chariots at top speed around the arena. They were allowed to ram and bump into each other, and chariots often overturned. Even though drivers wore protective clothing, they were sometimes killed. But the crowds loved chariot racing. They flocked to watch them in the thousands, and shouted and cheered as the chariots raced around.

When the emperors died, the Roman people worshiped them as gods. Christians refused to do this. So, from about A.D. 250, thousands of Christians were put in prison or thrown to the lions in front of watching crowds at an arena. In fear of their lives, Christians met in catacombs (undergound cemeteries, *left*) to pray in secret. In A.D. 313 emperor Constantine made Christianity legal.

GLADIATORS

Gladiators were slaves or criminals who were trained to fight to the death as the crowds looked on. They fought with shields and swords, or with tridents and nets. Gladiator fights and chariot races were both popular forms of entertainment. Rich citizens who wanted to be elected to office organized chariot races and gladiator fights that poor people could go to.

The emperor would often be present at gladiator fights. If a gladiator was wounded and asked for mercy, the emperor decided whether his life should be spared or not. If he had fought well, he was allowed to live. If not, the emperor signaled the victorious gladiator to kill him.

EMPERORS

Some Roman emperors were good rulers, like the first emperor, Augustus. He did not try to expand the empire but brought many years of peace to the people. Other emperors were brutal. Tiberius strengthened the empire but became a tyrant feared by all. His successor, Caligula, continued the reign of terror. Caligula was probably mad; he once made his horse a consul and had a palace built for it!

It is said that Nero, a vain man who saw himself as a great musician, played on the lyre as Rome burned.

One of the most cruel emperors was Nero, who was Caligula's nephew. In A.D. 64 a great fire destroyed part of Rome. Nero blamed the Christians and had many killed. In fact, he may have started the fire himself.

CHINA

THERE WAS a long period of unrest in China between 475 and 221 B.C. The Zhou *(see page 25)* were still in power but the separate states in China gradually became independent and began to fight each other.

China was united again under a powerful group of warriors, the Qin, who gradually subdued the power of the warring states and brought them under Qin rule. After many battles, the leader of the Qin assumed the role of emperor in 221 B.C. He called himself Qin Shi Huangdi, which means "first emperor of the Qin." Shi Huangdi ruled over a vast empire from his capital city, Xianyang.

Shi Huangdi was a ruthless, determined man but he had one great fear—death. In ancient times, people worshiped many different gods. Most people also believed in an afterlife. But this was the unknown and many feared what might happen to them. Shi Huangdi was no exception. Soon after he became emperor, he began to plan his tomb and 700,000 workers started to build it. The emperor wanted his tomb to be guarded by an army of 600,000 life-size soldiers made of clay.

The Qin emperor had to keep up a large army to protect his new empire. His warriors had bronze spears and swords, or fired arrows using a crossbow. An ordinary soldier was protected by body armor made of metal scales riveted together. He wore a scarf to prevent the armor rubbing his neck. His hair was coiled up into a top knot and tied with a scarf.

Shi Huangdi's terra-cotta army lay undisturbed for many hundreds of years until some Chinese laborers found some statues while digging a well. Archaeologists began to excavate the area and in 1974 they found the emperor's tomb. The army of warriors, some of them on horseback and carrying weapons, were well preserved and show us what soldiers looked like at the time. Each soldier has a different face, so they may have been portraits of the men in the emperor's real army.

The terra-cotta soldiers were originally painted in brilliant colors. These had faded by the time they were found.

THE GREAT WALL

Despite Shi Huangdi's power and his army, his empire was under constant threat from tribes such as the Huns, nomads who lived to the north of China. These fierce horsemen did not live in one place but moved around, raiding and plundering towns and villages, taking whatever they wanted and killing the inhabitants. Shi Huangdi decided to build a massive wall across China's northern border to keep the invaders out. By the time it was finished, the Great Wall of China stretched for 1,500 miles (2,400 km).

The Great Wall today.

When there was a threat of invasion at any part of the Great Wall, the nearest soldiers signaled to the others by lighting a fire. They rushed to help repel the invaders, firing arrows from the battlements and using catapults for hurling stones at enemies.

The Great Wall was an incredible construction for its time. Millions of men worked on building it and every piece of stone had to be carried to the site in baskets. The wall had towers every 650 feet (200 m), which were the living quarters of the soldiers who guarded it.

Shi Huangdi died suddenly in 210 B.C. and the Qin dynasty was taken over by a new dynasty, the Han, in 206. Work on the Great Wall went on for centuries after the death of the emperor who had started it. Most of the wall we see today was built between the 14th and the 16th centuries A.D., during the Ming dynasty. By the time the wall had been rebuilt and added to, it was 3,700 miles (6,000 km) long. It is 32 feet (10 m) high and wide enough for 10 men to march side by side along the top. It is still the largest structure ever built by people.

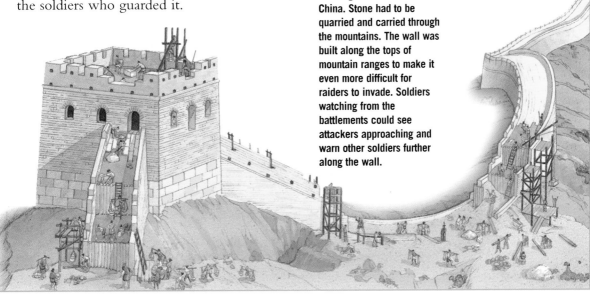

Building the Great Wall of China. Stone had to be quarried and carried through the mountains. The wall was built along the tops of mountain ranges to make it even more difficult for raiders to invade. Soldiers watching from the battlements could see attackers approaching and warn other soldiers further along the wall.

47

THE HAN EMPIRE

THE HAN DYNASTY ruled the Chinese empire for more than 400 years. This was a period of great prosperity for China. There were long periods of peace and the Chinese army added vast tracts of new land to the already powerful empire.

The teachings of Confucius *(see page 25)* became very important during this time. These stressed that it was better to govern people wisely than to rule them by force. Under the Han emperors, officials were instructed to help people as much as possible. This was also a time when scholars began to write histories of China.

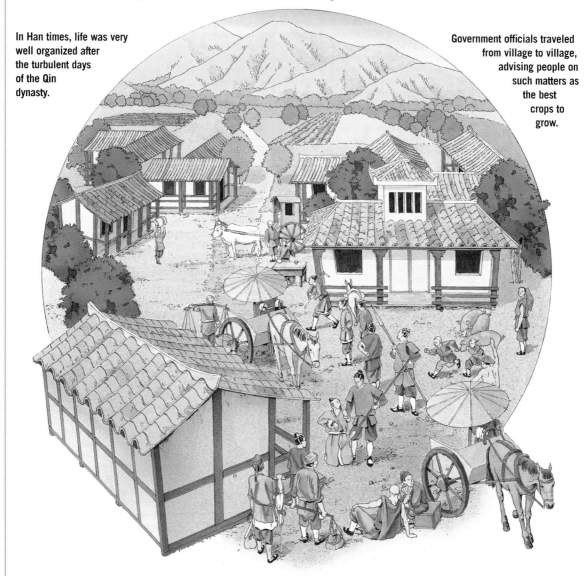

In Han times, life was very well organized after the turbulent days of the Qin dynasty.

Government officials traveled from village to village, advising people on such matters as the best crops to grow.

The Han period was a time of great technical achievement. The Chinese invented many things that we take for granted today. One of the most important inventions was paper, which was first manufactured in A.D. 105. The earliest paper was made from tree bark, old rags, and fishing nets pulped together with water, then flattened and dried in thin sheets.

Chinese scientists were the first to understand magnetism, and invented a compass more than 2,000 years ago. The stirrup was another early invention. Stirrups gave mounted soldiers more control over their horses and so helped them in battle. These and other inventions did not reach the West until hundreds of years later.

An early Chinese seismograph, a machine for recording earthquakes.

China was remote from the rest of the world for hundreds of years after the Han dynasty. Much of our knowledge about the Chinese way of life comes from models left in tombs. The Chinese were skilled craftspeople and made precious objects out of jade and bronze. Bronze models of horse-drawn chariots tell us what the full-size vehicles may have looked like. The chariots had two wheels and a canopy shaped like a parasol *(see illustration, opposite)*. Government officials rode in them when they traveled the countryside, inspecting villages. Models of buildings have also been found in tombs. Stone tomb slabs show scenes of everyday life in Han China.

The seismograph *(above)* was invented in A.D. 132. It is a vessel with eight dragons' heads around the bowl and toads sitting below. When the machine is shaken during an earthquake, a rod inside swings and opens one of the dragons' jaws. A ball falls out and drops into the mouth of the toad sitting directly below, recording the direction of the earthquake.

Another invention, the wheelbarrow *(see below)*, is in some ways an improvement on the type we use today. The Chinese wheelbarrow was invented in the first century B.C. The things being carried in the barrow are distributed on either side of a large wheel so that the weight is balanced. The barrow has long handles and is easier to push than modern versions.

This tiny bronze flying horse is an example of Han craft work.

A HAN CITY

The capital of the early Han empire was the city of Changan. The roads in the city were arranged on a grid system (they crossed each other at right angles). The traffic on the roads would have included two-wheeled chariots and goods wagons taking produce to market.

There were several marketplaces in the city, where people could buy food and materials such as silk, wood, and leather. Musicians, jugglers, and storytellers entertained people as they went about their business in the streets. The city was divided into sections, each one surrounded by a wall. Inside the walls, the houses were packed tightly together, protected from the bustle of the city.

THE SILK ROUTE

THE HAN CHINESE were traders whose merchants took silks from China to the West. An overland road, known as the Silk Route, linked cities in the Middle East to the early Han capital, Changan.

The Silk Route was about 4,000 miles (6,400 km) long and passed through dangerous territory where bandits waited to rob travelers. The merchants rode on camels and traveled in groups called caravans for protection. They carried silks, spices, and bronze articles to trade in the West.

The merchants came to various cities along the Silk Route and had to obtain permission to pass. The cities demanded a portion of the merchants' goods in payment before letting them through. So these cities became rich because of the Silk Route.

The illustration (below) shows a caravan of merchants setting out from China to travel to the West. Behind them is the Great Wall. The merchants' camels are followed by pack animals carrying the goods they are trading. The merchants will probably return with ivory, precious stones, horses, and other goods from the West.

As trade increased between East and West, more and more foreign merchants traveled to China, and many lived in Chang'an and other cities. Chang'an grew to be the largest city in the world.

It was through the merchants that some of China's secrets began to reach the West. Merchants would return to Europe with tales of what they had seen in this mysterious, unknown land, and some of the amazing things the people had invented.

Merchants continued to travel along the Silk Route for hundreds of years but it had become less important by about A.D. 1000. The cities along the route had become more and more powerful and could control the trade that passed through. There was always the threat of attack by bandits or groups of nomads who set upon the merchant caravans. As sea travel became safer and cheaper, that became the more popular way of transporting goods.

The Silk Route ran from Changan to cities in Central Asia and on to the Middle East. It passed between the high mountains of Tibet to the south and desert to the north.

INDIA

THE INDIAN civilization is one of the oldest in the world. Farmers had begun to build villages near the valley of the River Indus by about 6000 B.C. These settlements formed the basis of a civilization which developed from about 2400 B.C. The two capital cities of Harappa and Mohenjo Daro had streets of brick-built houses laid out on a grid system, and both cities had their own water and drainage systems. One of the first civilizations to have the wheel, the people also developed methods of writing.

Harappa and Mohenjo Daro flourished until about 1750 B.C., when all the people left them, perhaps because of years of severe flooding. The cities lay in ruins until 1922 when archaeologists began to excavate them and uncovered their remains.

By the 3rd century B.C. most of northern and central India had become one empire. This was called the Mauryan empire after Chandragupta Maurya, who founded it in 322 B.C. after Alexander the Great had left India *(see page 36)*.

Maurya, followed by his son Bindusara, brought most of the rest of India into the empire. By the time the third emperor, Asoka, came to power there was only one state left to conquer: Kalinga, on the east coast. Asoka managed to overthrow Kalinga, but caused so much bloodshed that he was overcome by guilt. He converted to the Buddhist religion and set about governing his empire in a more peaceful manner.

Asoka set up trading links with neighboring lands and built a network of roads. His beliefs about how people should behave and the laws he made were engraved on rocks and pillars throughout the empire.

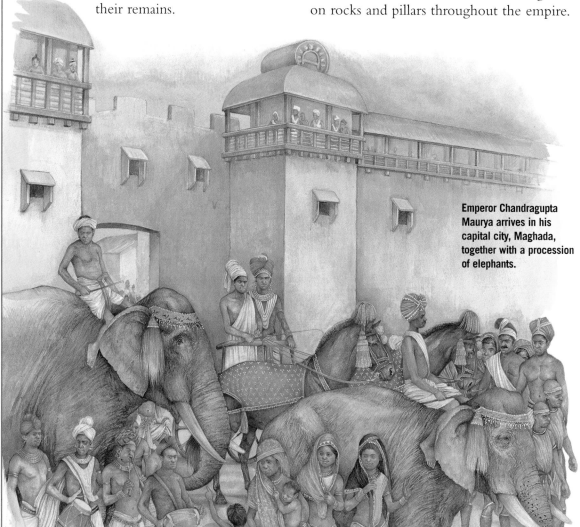

Emperor Chandragupta Maurya arrives in his capital city, Maghada, together with a procession of elephants.

Buddha found enlightenment as he sat under a fig tree.

HINDUISM AND BUDDHISM

When Asoka came to the throne, there were several different religions in India, including Hinduism, which later became India's main religion. Buddhism was founded by Siddhartha Gautama (c. 563–483 B.C.), but it only had small groups of followers until the reign of Asoka, who encouraged the spread of the religion throughout his empire. Siddhartha Gautama, who was later known as Buddha, was an Indian prince who became dissatisfied with the life of a nobleman. He left home to find a simpler and enlightened way of life.

When Buddha died, parts of his body were buried under mounds called stupas like this one, in different parts of India.

Siddhartha spent six years trying to find an answer to the sufferings of the world. Then one day he sat down under a fig tree (which came to be known as the Bo Tree or Tree of Enlightenment) and concentrated his mind. He sat there for 49 days, until he achieved enlightenment, a state of peace that was free from all human suffering.

Siddhartha became known as Buddha, "the enlightened one." He taught people how to live peaceful, good lives together by being unselfish and thinking of others. He also showed them how to meditate to find the meaning of life.

After Asoka's death, Hinduism became more popular again. Buddha was not a god and he was not worshiped as one. At first, there were not even statues of him. The Hindus believe that there is one supreme being, Brahman, who appears in the shape of many different gods and goddesses.

There are hundreds of Hindu gods and goddesses, but some are particularly important and featured in many festivals. The three most important gods are Brahma (above left), Vishnu (above right), and Shiva (right).

The three main gods are Brahma the Creator, Vishnu the Preserver, and Shiva the Destroyer. Shiva is sometimes also seen as a loving god. Vishnu appears in many forms, including Lord Krishna, who is worshiped as a holy child, as a mischievous youth, and as a brave warrior.

Buddhism and Hinduism became rival religions. Hindus had statues of their gods, so statues of a Buddha figure were introduced to make Buddhism more popular. The years of rivalry produced some of the finest sculpture in the world.

ANCIENT AMERICA

PEOPLE SETTLED in America quite recently compared to the other continents *(see page 8)*. They developed their civilizations independently from other parts of the world. They did not even know that there *were* other parts of the world.

People hunting mammoth, deer, and other animals, crossed into America from Asia between 35,000 and 15,000 years ago. It was the time of the Ice Age. Because so much water was frozen in ice caps, the sea levels were much lower than they are today. What is now the Bering Strait was then dry land. When the Ice Age ended, about 10,000 B.C., the ice melted and the sea level rose, cutting America off from elsewhere.

In some parts of the continent, people had to rely on plants rather than animals for food. The first farmers worked the land in what is now Mexico and Peru.

Giant stone heads like this one were carved by the Olmecs, the first civilization in Mexico. Each head weighs up to 22 tons (20 tonnes). The heads look similar but they are all different and are portraits of Olmec rulers. The pattern on the helmet shows who the ruler is.

THE OLMECS

The Olmecs lived in the swampy lands near the Gulf of Mexico. They developed their civilization from about 1200 B.C. The people were artists and traders who did not seek to conquer other parts of America. They worshiped gods and built pyramid temples, a style that was adopted by later Mexican civilizations.

Olmec traders traveled far and wide within Mexico, searching for raw materials, such as jade, for their craft work, and trading in the finished products. Their travels brought them into contact with other peoples who were influenced by their art. The Olmec civilization faded in about 300 B.C.

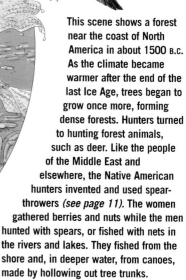

This scene shows a forest near the coast of North America in about 1500 B.C. As the climate became warmer after the end of the last Ice Age, trees began to grow once more, forming dense forests. Hunters turned to hunting forest animals, such as deer. Like the people of the Middle East and elsewhere, the Native American hunters invented and used spear-throwers *(see page 11)*. The women gathered berries and nuts while the men hunted with spears, or fished with nets in the rivers and lakes. They fished from the shore and, in deeper water, from canoes, made by hollowing out tree trunks.

TEOTIHUACÁN

The next major development in Mexican civilization was the building of the great city of Teotihuacán (about 30 miles [50 km] from present-day Mexico City). The site of Teotihuacán was a place of pilgrimage: a cave, said to be the birthplace of the sun. The huge Pyramid of the Sun was built over this cave in the 1st century A.D. and a magnificent city was laid out around it. The pyramid can still be seen today.

At its peak, about 200,000 people lived in Teotihuacá n. It was one of the largest cities in the world. Wealthy people lived near the center, while farmers and craftspeople had simpler homes on the outskirts.

Warrior-priests were the lords of Moche society. They dressed in elaborate finery and head-dresses, and wore priceless gold jewelry.

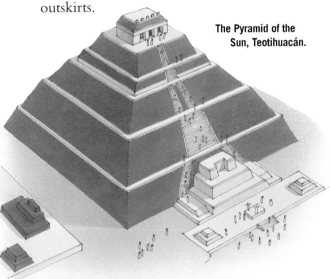

The Pyramid of the Sun, Teotihuacán.

Teotihuacán was destroyed in A.D. 750 and all its inhabitants moved away. But it remained a place of pilgrimage. It probably influenced the Aztecs when they built their city of Tenochtitlán hundreds of years later.

The Moche were brilliant potters and metalworkers who built up a kingdom of thousands of people. Their civilization lasted for 800 years until A.D. 800. Moche rulers were warrior-priests who were extremely rich and powerful. They led their armies out to conquer neighboring peoples and presided over the sacrifice of prisoners to the gods.

The Moche traded with other peoples in Peru. Among these were the Nazca, who lived on the edge of the desert further south. The Nazca people carved hundreds of lines in the desert's sandy surface, and a series of strange pictures, including images of birds, monkeys, spiders, and others. They can only be properly seen from the air. Why the Nazca people made these lines and pictures—long before planes were invented—remains a mystery.

PERUVIAN KINGDOMS

A giant pyramid was also built by the Moche people of Peru in South America. This was the Huaca del Sol (also known as the Pyramid of the Sun), which towered 135 feet (41 m) above the plains on which it stood. On its summit were palaces, temples, and shrines. More than 143 million mud bricks were used to build this massive structure.

No one knows what the Nazca pictures mean, but they may have played a part in a religious ritual.

AFRICA

THE EARLIEST forms of art in Africa are paintings left on rocks in the Sahara desert, a green and fertile region 8,000 years ago. Bands of hunter-gatherers lived there, but as the Sahara dried up they moved away. Some went east to found the ancient Egyptian civilization *(see page 16)*. Others moved south.

By about 500 B.C. some people had learned to mine and work metals such as iron. As they spread over Africa, they took this knowledge with them.

The earliest examples of African sculpture were found at Nok in Nigeria. These terracotta heads and figures date from between 500 B.C. and A.D. 200. They may have inspired artists of a later civilization at Ife in Nigeria.

The Nok people found out about ironworking in around 400 BC, probably from traders crosssing the Sahara desert. Iron was perfect for making axes—used for felling trees—and farming tools. It was smelted (separated from the rock) in a clay furnace. Bellows were used to make the fire hot enough to melt the iron. The molten metal ran into a pit underneath the fire.

OCEANIA

OCEANIA consists of the islands of Australia and New Zealand, Papua New Guinea, and the other South Pacific islands. The first to be settled were Australia and New Guinea. The people who became the Aborigine migrated to Australia from Southeast Asia probably about 50,000 years ago. People from Asia also settled on New Guinea about 40,000 years ago.

The other islands were not settled until about 5,000 years ago. New Zealand remained uninhabited only until about 1,000 years ago. Finding these islands in ancient times involved the risky business of traveling very long distances in canoes. The first settlers were skilled seafarers.

The Aborigine believed in an everlasting spiritual life known as "Eternal Dreaming." Their music, poetry, dancing, and sculpture were all inspired by their religious beliefs. One musical instrument was a long wooden tube called a didgeridoo. The weather was very important to the Aborigine. Many of their rituals involved the fertility of the land and the growth of new plants.

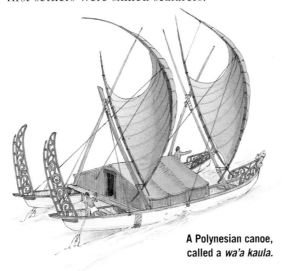

A Polynesian canoe, called a *wa'a kaula*.

Polynesia consists of many islands spread thousands of miles apart across the Pacific Ocean. The ancestors of today's Polynesians constructed large canoes, some big enough to hold 100 people, to explore and settle these islands. Groups of people came from the mainland of Asia and found their way across the sea by observing the stars. Discovery of the islands was gradual and it was several thousand years before they were all inhabited.

The Aborigine of Australia were hunter-gatherers, but the people of New Guinea became farmers about 9,000 years ago. There is evidence that they grew yams, coconuts, bananas, and sugarcane.

Easter Island lies 2,300 miles (3,700 km) off the coast of Chile, South America. There are about 600 massive stone heads dotted about on the island. Who built them, and how and why they did so, remains a mystery.

Settlers probably reached Easter Island between A.D. 400 and 500. They built long altar platforms on the seashore where religious rituals took place. The heads were not carved until later. They stood on the altars, facing inland, but they were probably not statues of gods. They are more likely to be ancestors of the island's inhabitants.

The statues were carved at the quarries where the stone came from—only the eyes were added once the statues were in position. No one really knows how these huge blocks of stone were put in place.

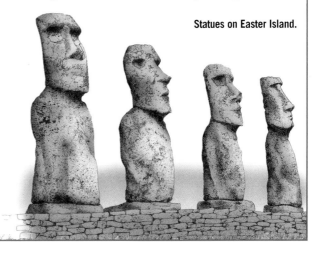

Statues on Easter Island.

TIMELINE I

c.4.4 million B.C. Australopithecines, the first humanlike creatures to walk upright, appear.

c.2.5 million *Homo habilis* ("handy man") appears in Africa. It uses simple tools. The start of the Palaeolithic or Old Stone Age.

c.1.8 million *Homo erectus* ("upright man") appears in Africa. It uses sharper tools and fire.

c.750,000 *Homo sapiens* ("wise man") appears in Africa. These people later spread out into other parts of the world, including China and Indonesia.

c.200,000 The first Neanderthal people appear.

c.125,000 The first modern people, *Homo sapiens sapiens,* appear in Africa.

c.60,000 People first arrive in Australia.

c.40,000 *Homo sapiens sapiens* reaches Europe.

c.35,000 The first people begin to cross into America.

c.30,000 Neanderthals die out.

c.10,000 The end of the Ice Age (or its latest coldest phase). The start of the Neolithic period, or New Stone Age. Farming begins in Mesopotamia. Some animals are domesticated for the first time.

c.8350 The founding of Jericho, the first walled town in the world.

c.7000 Çatal Hüyük, probably the largest city of its day, is built in Turkey.

c.7000 Farming of root crops begins in New Guinea.

c.6500 Farming in Greece and the Aegean spreads up the River Danube to Hungary by about 5500.

c.6000 The Minoans arrive on Crete.

c.6000 Rice cultivation begins (Thailand).

c.5000 The first farming communities settle by the Nile River in Egypt.

c.5000 Groups of farmers begin irrigation in Mesopotamia.

c.5000 People in southeast Europe make copper and gold objects.

c.5000 The Chinese civilization begins. Farming communities settle in the Indus valley in India.

c.4500 Scratch plough first used (in Mesopotamia).

c.4500 Farming spreads to most other parts of western Europe.

c.3750 The start of bronze-casting in the Near East.

c.3500 Early writing develops in Mesopotamia.

c.3400 Egypt has developed as two kingdoms, Upper and Lower Egypt.

c.3200 Wooden wheels, made from planks pegged together, in use in Mesopotamia.

c.3100 Egypt is united under the first pharaoh, Menes. The Egyptians are the first people in the ancient world to form a unified nation (other civilizations consist of separate city-states).

c.3000 The spread of copper-working in Europe.

c.3000 The development of major cities, such as Ur, in Sumer.

c.3000 Arable farming spreads to central Africa.

c.3000 First pottery made in the Americas.

c.2800 Construction work begins on Stonehenge, a stone monument in England.

c.2575 The start of the Old Kingdom in Egypt. Powerful pharaohs send out trading expeditions to find treasures to bring back. Work begins on the pyramids at Giza. They become one of the Seven Wonders of the Ancient World. Local nobles become more

and more rich and powerful. Eventually, unified rule of Egypt collapses and civil war for the next 100 years brings the Old Kingdom to an end in 2134.

c.2500 The rise of the Assyrian civilization in northern Mesopotamia. The Assyrians adopt the religion and culture of Sumer.

c.2400 The Indian civilization develops, with Mohenjo Daro and Harappa as its major cities.

c.2370–2230 Sargon I of Akkad (to the north of Sumer) founds the first empire in the Middle East by taking control of the Sumerian region and leading his armies into Anatolia and Syria.

c.2300 Bronze Age in Europe begins.

c.2100 The Hebrews, led by Abraham, settle in Canaan on the eastern Mediterranean coast.

c.2040 The start of the Middle Kingdom in Egypt. The country is united under a king from Thebes, Mentuhotep. Hyksos invaders begin to arrive from Syria from about 1730. They gradually gain control of Egypt (there are at least five Hyksos kings of Egypt). The Middle Kingdom ends in chaos in 1640 B.C.

c.2000 The Minoan civilization begins on Crete with the building of palaces.

c.2000 Metal-working begins in Peru.

c.2000 Sea-going ships with sails are developed in the Aegean.

c.1792 King Hammurabi comes to the throne of Babylon, which now begins to dominate Mesopotamia as Hammurabi builds up his empire.

c.1750 The Indus Valley civilization comes to an end.

c.1750 The Shang dynasty comes to power in China.

c.1650 The start of the Hittite Empire. The Hittites settled Anatolia (present-day Turkey)

in c.2000 B.C. Under King Hattushili I, they conquer northern Syria.

c.1600 A great famine drives the Hebrews from Canaan to Egypt.

c.1595 Hittites overthrow Babylonian empire.

c.1560 The Theban prince Ahmose drives the Hyksos from Egypt and the New Kingdom begins. During this period, Egypt controls Nubia to the south and much of Syria and Canaan. Pharaohs are no longer buried in pyramids but in smaller tombs in the Valley of the Kings.

c.1550 The Mycenaean civilization begins in Greece.

c.1500 Complex communities led by chieftains develop in Europe.

c.1500 Writing develops both in China and Greece.

c.1450 The Minoan civilization disappears.

c.1377 Akhenaten, pharaoh of Egypt, enforces the worship of a single god, Aten.

c.1290 Rameses II (Rameses the Great) comes to the throne of Egypt and reigns for 67 years. The Hittites wage war on the Egyptians during his reign and fight them at the Battle of Qadesh. Although neither side wins, Rameses records the battle as a victory for Egypt.

c.1270 The Hebrews leave Egypt (the "Exodus") and settle in Canaan.

c.1200 The Hittite empire collapses.

c.1200 Egypt is attacked by groups of raiders called the "Sea People," who are defeated by the army of the pharaoh Rameses III. Some Sea People settle in Canaan. They become known as the Philistines.

c.1200 The Mycenaean civilization in Greece collapses.

c.1200 The Olmec civilization begins in Mexico.

TIMELINE II

c.1160 B.C. The death of Rameses III, the last great pharoah of Egypt.

c.1100 The Shang dynasty is overthrown in China. The Zhou dynasty begins.

c.1100–850 The Dark Ages in Greece.

c.1000 The Phoenicians expand their influence in the Mediterranean region. They develop an alphabet script, the basis of modern western European scripts.

c.1000 King David unites Israel and Judah.

814 A Phoenician colony is founded at Carthage, North Africa.

c.800 The Etruscan civilization begins in Italy.

c.800 City-states are founded in Greece.

753 The traditional date for the founding of Rome.

c.750 Homer writes the *Iliad* and later the *Odyssey*.

776 The first Olympic Games are held in Greece.

671 The Assyrians conquer Egypt.

650 Iron technology is introduced in China

625 King Nabopolassar overthrows the Assyrians and Babylon is powerful again.

563 The birth of Siddhartha Gautama (Buddha) in India.

c.560 The rise of the Persian empire under Cyrus II (Cyrus the Great)

551 The birth of the philosopher Confucius in China.

521 The Persian empire expands under Darius I (Darius the Great). It stretches from Egypt to India.

510 Tarquin the Proud, the last king of Rome, is driven out and Rome becomes a republic with two classes, the patricians (nobles) and the plebeians (workers).

c.500 The dawn of the Classical Age in Greece and the start of democratic government. Each city-state has its own army, although only Sparta's is full time.

c.500 The start of Nok culture in Nigeria, Africa. The Nok provide what are thought to be the first examples of African sculpture.

490 The Persians invade Greece and raid Athens. They are defeated at the Battle of Marathon.

c.483 The death of Buddha.

480 The Persian fleet is defeated by the Athenians at the Battle of Salamis.

479 The Greeks defeat the Persians at Plataea. This victory marks the end of the Persian invasions on Greece.

479 The death of Confucius in China.

449 The Greeks make peace with Persia. Athens begins to flourish under its new leader, Pericles. The Parthenon is built.

431–404 The Peloponnesian Wars are fought between Athens and Sparta. Athens surrenders to Sparta, which attempts to found an empire.

391 The Gauls attack Rome but are bribed with gold to leave.

371 The Spartans are defeated by General Epaminondas from the city-state of Thebes. This puts an end to Spartan rule.

359 Philip becomes king of Macedonia in northern Greece.

338 Philip of Macedonia defeats the Greeks at the Battle of Chaerona and unites Greece under his rule.

336 Philip is murdered and his son Alexander becomes king of Macedonia.

334 Alexander the Great invades Persia and defeats Darius III.

326 Alexander conquers northern India.

323 Alexander dies in Babylon. The Hellenistic period begins in Greece.

322 The Mauryan empire is founded in India by Chandragupta Maurya.

304 Ptolemy I, Macedonian governor of Egypt, founds a new dynasty of pharaohs.

300 The Olmec civilization disappears in Mexico.

290 Rome completes its conquest of central Italy by defeating the Samnites from the west.

290 The library is founded at Alexandria

264–41 The First Punic War with Carthage gives Rome control of Sicily.

262 Asoka, the Mauryan emperor (rules 272–236) converts to Buddhism.

221 Qin rule begins in China. Shi Huangdi becomes the first emperor. Work on the Great Wall of China begins.

218–201 The Second Punic War. Hannibal of Carthage invades Italy by marching with 36 elephants across the Alps.

210 Shi Huangdi of China dies. The Han dynasty begins.

206 Rome gains control of Spain.

149–46 The Third Punic War. Rome destroys Carthage. North Africa becomes a Roman province.

146 Greece is dominated by Rome.

141 The Chinese emperor, Wu Ti, expands the power of the Han dynasty across eastern Asia.

c.112 The Silk Route is opened, linking China to the West.

c.100 The Moche civilization begins in Peru.

73 The gladiator Spartacus leads a slaves' revolt in Rome. Spartacus is killed by the Roman army.

59 Julius Caesar is elected consul of Rome.

58–49 Julius Caesar conquers Gaul and invades Britain twice.

46 Julius Caesar rules Rome as a dictator. Cleopatra is made queen of Egypt.

44 Julius Caesar is stabbed to death by Brutus and a group of senators.

43 Mark Antony and Octavian, Caesar's nephew, come to power in Rome.

31 Octavian defeats Antony and Cleopatra at the Battle of Actium.

30 The death of Antony and Cleopatra.

27 Octavian becomes Augustus, the first emperor of Rome.

c.5 The birth of Jesus Christ, the founder of Christianity.

1st century A.D. The city of Teotihuacán is built in Mexico.

A.D. 14 Augustus dies and his stepson Tiberius becomes emperor of Rome.

c.30 Jesus Christ is crucified in Jerusalem.

37 Caligula becomes emperor of Rome upon the death of Tiberius.

41 Caligula is murdered and his uncle, Claudius, becomes emperor of Rome.

54 Claudius is poisoned by his wife. Her son Nero becomes emperor.

64 Fire destroys part of Rome.

79 Pompeii and Herculaneum are destroyed by the eruption of Vesuvius.

117 The Roman Empire is at its greatest extent. Hadrian becomes emperor.

c.300 The rise of the Hopewell Indian chiefdoms in North America

313 Christianity becomes the official religion of the Roman Empire under the emperor Constantine.

330 Constantinople (now Istanbul, Turkey) becomes the capital of the Roman Empire.

400 Settlers reach Easter Island.

410 The barbarian Visigoths invade Italy and sack Rome.